The Hekatompathia

Or

Passionate Centurie Of Love

by
Thomas Watson

To the Right Honorable my very good Lord Edward de Vere, Earle of Oxenford, Viscount Bulbecke, Lord of Escales, and Badlesmere, and Lord High Chamberlain of England, all happinesse.

Alexander the Great, passing on a time by the workshop of Apelles, curiously surveyed some of his doings, whose long stay in viewing them brought all the people into so great a good liking of the painter's workmanship, that immediately after they bought up all his pictures, what price soever he set them at.

And the like good hap (Right Honorable) befell unto me lately concerning these my Love Passions, which then chanced to Apelles for his Portraits. For since the world hath understood (I know not how) that your Honor had willingly vouchsafed the acceptance of this work, and at convenient leisures favorably perused it, being as yet but in written hand, many have oftentimes and earnestly called upon me to put it to the press, that for their money they might but see what your Lordship with some liking had already perused. And therewithal some of them said (either to yield your Honor his due praise, for soundness of judgment; or to please me, of whom long since they had conceived well) that Alexander would like of no lines, but such as were drawn by the cunning hand, and with the curious pencil, of Apelles. Which I set not down here to that end, that I would confer my Poems with Apelle's Portraits for worthiness; albeit I fitly compare your Honor's person with Alexander's for excellence. But how bold soever I have been in turning out this my petty poor flock upon the open Common of the wide world, where every man may behold their nakedness, I humbly make request that if any storm fall unlooked-for (by the fault of malicious high foreheads or the poison of evil-edged tongues) these my little ones may shroud themselves under the broad-leafed Platane of your Honor's patronage. And thus at this present, I humbly take my leave; but first wishing the continual increase of your Lordship's honor, with abundance of true Friends, reconciliation of all Foes, and what good soever tendeth unto perfect happiness.

Your Lordship's humbly at command

Thomas VVatson

To the friendly Reader.

Courteous Reader, if any thing herein either please or profit thee, afford me thy good word in recompense of my pains: if ought offend or hurt thee, I desire that thou forget the one and forgive the other. This toy being liked, the next may prove better; being discouraged, will cut off the likelihood of my travail to come. But by that means all will be well, and both parties pleased. For neither shall I repent my labor in the like, nor thou be any more troubled with my faults or follies.

Yet for this once I hope that thou wilt in respect of my travail in penning these love-passions, or for pity of my pains in suffering them (although but supposed) so survey the faults herein escaped, as either to wink at them, as oversights of a blind Lover; or to excuse them, as idle toys proceeding from a youngling frenzy; or lastly, to defend them by saying, it is nothing *Praeter decorum* for a maimed man to halt in his pace, where his wound enforceth him, or for a Poet to falter in his Poem when his matter requireth it. *Homer*, in mentioning the swiftness of the wind, maketh his verse to run in post-haste all upon *Dactilus*: and *Virgil* in expressing the striking-down of an ox, letteth the end of his hexameter fall withal, *Procumbit* humi bos.

Therefore, if I rough-hewed my verse, where my sense was unsettled, whether through the nature of the passion, which I felt, or by rule of art, which I had learned, it may seem a happy fault; or if it were so framed by counsel, thou mayest think it well done; if by chance, happily.

Yet write I not this to excuse myself of such errors, as are escaped either by dotage, or ignorance; but those I refer to thy gentle courtesy and favorable construction, or lay many of them upon the Printer's neck, whom I would blame by his own press, if he would suffer me.

As for any Aristarchus, Momus, or Zoilus, if they pinch me more than is reasonable, thou courteous Reader, which art of a better disposition, shalt rebuke them in my behalf; saying to the first that my birds are all of mine own hatching and that my only over-much haste made Sol angry in their Birthday; to the second, that although Venus be in my verse, yet her slipper is left out; to the last and worst, that I rather take upon me to write better than Chaerilus, than once suppose to imitate Homer.

I am over-long, as well for the fear I had to be bitten by such as are captious, as for the desire I have to please thee that art friendly. But since I now well remember me, that nothing is more easily let flown, nothing sooner dispersed, nothing later recalled back again, than the bitter blast of an evil-spoken man, and that he whom it shall hurt had no recure but by patience; I will set it behind my heel as a hurt remedyless, or else, when it comes, salve it up with patience.

In the mean space (courteous Reader) I once again crave the favorable judgment: and so, for brevity's sake, abruptly make an end; committing thee to God, and my work to thy favor.

Thine, as thou art his,
Thomas Watson.

John Lyly to the Author his friend

My good friend, I have read your new passions, and they have renewed mine old pleasures, the which brought to me no less delight than they have done to yourself commendations. And certes had not one of mine eyes about serious affairs been watchful, both by being too too busy had been wanton: such is the nature of persuading pleasure, that it melteth the marrow before it scorch the skin, and burneth before it warmeth: Not unlike unto the oil of *Jeat*, which rotteth the bone and never rankleth the flesh, or the Scarab flies, which enter into the root and never touch the rind.

And whereas you desire to have my opinion, you may imagine that my stomach is rather cloyed than queasy, and therefore mine appetite of less force than mine affection, fearing rather a surfeit of sweetness than desiring a satisfying. The repeating of Love wrought in me a remembrance of liking, but searching the very veins of my heart, I could find nothing but a broad scar where I left a deep wound: and loose string, where I tied hard knots: and a table of steel where I framed a plot of wax.

Whereby I noted that young swans are gray and the old white, young trees tender and the old tough, young men amorous, and growing in years, either wiser or warier. The Coral in the water is a soft weed, on the land a hard stone: a sword frieth in the fire like a black eel, but laid in earth like white snow: the heart in love is altogether passionate but free from desire, altogether careless.

But it is not my intent to inveigh against love, which women account but a bare word, and that men reverence as the best God: only this I would add without offense to Gentlewomen, that were not men more superstitious in their praises, than women are constant in their passions: Love would either shortly be worn out of use, or men out of love, or women out of lightness. I can condemn none but by conjecture, nor commend any but by lying, yet suspicion is as free as thought, and as far as I see as necessary as credulity.

Touching your Mistress I must needs think well, seeing you have written so well, but as false glasses show the fairest faces, so fine glozes amend the baddest fancies. Apelles straight leg, whom nature framed with a poult-foot, which proveth men to be of greater affection their judgment. But in that so aptly you have varied upon women, I will not vary from you, so confess I must, and if I should not, yet mought I be compelled, that to Love were the sweetest thing in the earth: If women were the faithfullest, and that women would be more constant if men were more wise. And seeing you have used me so friendly, as to make me acquainted with your passions, I will shortly make you privy to mine, which I would be loath the printer should see, for that my fancies being never so crooked, he would put them in straight lines, unfit for my humor, necessary for his art, who setteth down, blind, in as many letters as seeing.

Farewell.

A Quatorzain, in the commendation of Master Thomas Watson, and of his Mistress, for whom he wrote this Book of Passionate Sonnets.

The stars, which did at Petrarch's birthday reign,
Were fix'd again at thy nativity,
Destining thee the Tuscan's poesy,
Who scaled the skies in lofty Quatorzain,
The Muses gave to thee thy fatal vein,
The very fame that Petrarch had, whereby
Madonna Laura's fame is grown so high,
And that whereby his glory he did gain.
Thou hast a Laura, whom well thou dost commend,
And to her praise thy passion songs do tend;
Ye both such praise deserve, as naught can smother;
In brief, with Petrarch and his Laura in grace
Thou and thy Dame be equal, save percase
Thou pass the one, and she excels the other.

G. Bucke.

To the Author.

Thy book beginning sweet and ending sour,
Dear friend, bewrays thy false success in love,
Where smiling first, thy Mistress falls to lower,
When thou did'st hope her courtesy to prove;
And finding thy expected luck to fail,
Thou fall'st from praise, and dost begin to rail.
To use great terms in praise of thy device,
I think were vain: therefore I leave them out;
Content thee, that the Censure of the wise
Hath put that needless question out of doubt:
Yet how I weight the work that thou hast wrought,
My judgment I refer unto thy thought.

T. Acheley.

An Ode,
Written to the Muses,
Concerning this Author.

You sacred Nymphs, Apollo's sisters fair,
Daughters of Jove, parents of rare device,
Why take you no delight in change of air?
Is Helicon your only paradise?
Hath Britain soil no hill, no heath, no well,
No weed, no wit, wherein you list to dwell?
Ladies vouchsafe with patience once to view
Our lively springs, high hills, and pleasant shades,
And as you like the seat and country's hue,
Pitch down your tents, and use your sporting trades;
Hard hap it is, if nothing here you find
That you can deem delightful to your mind.
Lo Watson press'd to entertain your power
In pleasant springs of flowing wit and skill;
If you esteem the pleasures of his bower,
Let Britain bear your spring, your grove and hill,
That it hence forth may of your favor boast,
And him, whom first you here vouchsafe for host.

C. Downhalus.

It's seldom seen that Merit hath his due,
Or else Desert to find his just desire:
For now Reproof with his defacing crew
Treads underfoot that rightly should aspire:
Mild Industry discourag'd hides his face,
And shuns the light, in fear to meet *Disgrace*.
Seld seen said I (yet always seen with some)
That Merit gains good will, a golden hire,
With whom *Reproof* is cast aside for scum;
That grows apace that virtue helps t' aspire;
And Industry well cherish'd to his face
In sunshine walks, in spite of sour *Disgrace*.
This favor hath put life into the pen,
That here presents his first fruit in this kind;
He hopes acceptance, friendly grant it then;
Perchance some better work doth stay behind.
My censure is, which reading you shall see,
A *Pithy, sweet,* and cunning poesy.

M. Royden.

To the Author

IF graver heads shall count it over-light,
To treat of *Love*: say thou to them: *A stain*
Is incident unto the finest die.
And yet no stain at all it is for thee,
These lays of *Love*, as mirth to melancholy,
To follow fast thy sad *Antigone*,
Which may bear out a broader work than this,
Compil'd with judgment, order, and with art.
And shroud thee under shadow of his wings,
Whose gentle heart, and head with learning fraught
Shall yield thee gracious favor and defense.

G. Peele.

A Quatorzain of the Authour unto this his booke of Lovepassions.

My little book go hie thee hence away,
Whose price (God knows) will countervail no part
Of pains I took to make thee what thou art:
And yet I joy thy birth. But hence I say,
Thy brothers are half hurt by thy delay;
For thou thyself art like the deadly dart,
Which bred thy birth from out my wounded heart.
But still observe this rule where ere thou stay,
In all thou may'st tender thy father's fame,
Bad is the Bird that filleth his own nest.
If thou be much mislik'd, They are to blame,
Say thou, that deeds well done to evil rest:
Or else confess, *A Toy* to be thy name;
This trifling world *A Toy* beseemeth best.

The Hekatompathia

Or

Passionate Centurie Of Love

I.

The Author in this Passion taketh but occasion to open his estate in love; the miserable accidents whereof are sufficiently described hereafter in the copious variety of his devices: and whereas in this Sonnet he seemeth one while to despair, and yet by and by after to hav some hope of good success, the contrariety ought not to offend, if the nature and true quality of a love passion be well considered. And where he mentioneth that once he scorned love, he alludeth to a piece of work which he wrote long since, *De Romedio Amoris*, which he hath lately perfected, to the good liking of many that have seen and perused it, though not fully to his own fancy, which causeth him as yet to keep it back from the print.

Well fare the life sometimes I led ere this,
When yet no downy hair yclad my face:
My heart devoid of cares did bathe in bliss,
My thoughts were free in every time and place;
  But now (alas) all's foul, which then was fair,
  My wonted joys are turning to despair.
Where then I liv'd without control or check,
Another now is mistress of my mind,
Cupid hath clapt a yoke upon my neck,
Under whose weight I live in servile kind:
  I now cry creak, that ere I scorned love,
  Whose might is more than other Gods above.
I have essayed by labor to eschew
What fancy builds upon a love conceit,
But ne'ertheless my thought revives anew,
Where in fond love is wrapt, and works deceit:
  Some comfort yet I have to live her thrall,
  In whom as yet I find no fault at all.

II.

In this passion the Author describeth in how piteous a case the heart of a lover is, being (as he feigneth here) separated from his own body, and removed into a darksome and solitary wilderness of woes. The conveyance of his invention is plain and pleasant enough of itself, and therefore needeth the less annotation before it.

My heart is set him down twixt hope and fears
Upon the stony bank of high desire,
To view his own made flood of blubbering tears
Whose waves are bitter salt, and hot as fire:
  There blows no blast of wind but ghostly groans
  Nor waves make other noise than piteous moans
As life were spent he waiteth Charon's boat,
And thinks he dwells on side of Stygian lake:
But black despair sometimes with open throat,
Or spiteful jealousy doth cause him quake,
  With howling shrieks on him they call and cry
  That he as yet shall neither live nor die;
Thus void of help he fits in heavy case,
And wanteth voice to make his just complaint.
No flower but Hyacinth in all the place,
No sun comes there, nor any heav'nly saint,
  But only she, which in himself remains,
  And joys her ease though he abound in pains.

III.

This passion is all framed in manner of a dialogue, wherein the Author talketh with his own heart, being now through the commandment and force of love separated from his body miraculously, and against nature, to follow his mistress in hope, by long attendance upon her, to purchase in the end her love and favor, and by that means to make himself all one with her own heart.

Speak gentle heart, where is thy dwelling place?
With her, whose birth the heavens themselves have blest.
What dost thou there? Sometimes behold her face,
And lodge sometimes within her crystal breast:
  She cold, thou hot, how can you then agree?
  Not nature now, but love doth govern me.
With her wilt thou remain, and let me die?
If I return, we both shall die for grief;
If still thou stay, what good shall grow thereby?
I'll move her heart to purchase thy relief;
  What if her heart be hard and stop his cares?
  I'll sigh aloud and make him soft with tears:
If that prevail, wilt thou return from thence?
Not I alone, her heart shall come with me:
Then will you both live under my defense?
So long as life will let us both agree:
  Why then despair, go pack thee hence away,
  I live in hope to have a golden day.

IIII.

The chief ground and matter of this Sonnet standeth upon the rehearsal of such things as by report of the Poets, are dedicated unto Venus, whereof the Author sometime wrote these three Latin verses.

Mons Erycinus, Acidalius fons, alba columba,
Hesperus, ora Pathos, Rofa, Myrtus, et insula Cyprus,
Idaliumque nemus; Veneri haec sunt omnia sacra.

And *Forcatulus* the French Poet wrote upon the fame particulars, but more at large, he beginneth thus,

Est arbor Veneri Myrtus gratissima, flores
Tam Rosa, quam volucres alba columba praeit.
Igniserum coeli prae cunctis diligit astris
Hesperon, Idalium, soepe, adit una nemus, etc.

Sweet Venus, if as now thou stand my friend,
As once thou did'st unto King Priam's son,
My joyful muse shall never make an end
Of praising thee, and all that thou hast done:
Nor this my pen shall ever cease to write
  Of ought, wherein sweet Venus takes delight.
  My temples hedged in with Myrtle boughs
Shall set aside Apelles Laurel tree,
As did Anchises' son, when both his brows[1]
With Myrtle he beset, to honor thee:
  Then will I say, the Rose of flowers is best.
  And silver Doves for birds excel the rest.
I'll praise no star but Hesperus alone,
Nor any hill but Erycinus mount,
Nor any wood but Idaly alone,
Nor any spring but Acidalian fount,
  Nor any land but only Cyprus shore,
  Nor Gods but Love, and what would Venus more?

1. Materna redimitus tempora Mirto. Virg.

V. & VI.

All this Passion (two verses only excepted) is wholly translated out of Petrarch, where he writeth,

S' amor non e, che dunque e quel ch'i sento? . . Part prima }
Ma s egli e amor, per Dio che cosa, e quale? . . Sonnet 103}
Se buona, ond'e l'effetto aspro e mortale?
Se ria, ond' e si dolce ogni tormento?

Herein certain contrarieties, which are incident to him that loveth extremely, are lively expressed by a Metaphor. And it may be noted that the Author in his first half verse of this translation varieth from that sense which Chaucer useth in translating the self same; which he doth upon no other warrant than his own simple private opinion, which yet he will not greatly stand upon.

If't be not love I feel, what is it then?
If love it be, what kind a thing is love?
If good, how chance he hurts so many men?
If bad, how haps that none his hurts disprove?
  If willingly I burn, how chance I wail?
  If gainst my will, what sorrow will avail?
O livesome death, O sweet and pleasant ill,
Against my mind how can thy might prevail?
If I bend back, and but refrain my will,
If I consent, I do not well to wail;
  {And touching him, whom will hath made a slave,
  The Proverb say'th of old, *Self do, self have.*}[1]
Thus being toss'd with winds of sundry sort
Through dang'rous Seas but in a slender Boat,
With error stuff'd, and driv'n beside the port,
Where void of wisdom's freight it lies afloat.
  I wave in doubt what help I shall require,
  In Summer freeze, in winter burn like fire.

1. Adduntur Tuscano hij duo versus.

VII.

This passion of love is lively expressed by the Author, in that he lavishly praiseth the person and beautiful ornaments of his love, one after another as they lie in order. He partly imitateth herein Aeneas Silvius, who setteth down the like in describing Lucretia the love of Euryalus; and partly he followeth Ariosto cant. 7, where he describeth Alcina; and partly borroweth from some others where they describe the famous Helen of Greece: you may therefore, if you please aptly call this sonnet as a Scholar of good judgment hath already Christened it *ainh parasitikh.*[1]

Hark you that list to hear what saint I serve:
Her yellow locks exceed the beaten gold;
Her sparkling eyes in heav'n a place deserve;
Her forehead high and fair of comely mold;
  Her words are music all of silver sound;
  Her wit so sharp as like can scarce be found;
Each eyebrow hangs like Iris in the skies;
Her Eagle's nose is straight of stately frame;[2]
On either cheek a Rose and Lily lies;
Her breath is sweet perfume, or holy flame;
  Her lips more red than any Coral stone;
  Her neck more white than aged Swans that moan;[3]
Her breast transparent is, like Crystal rock;
Her fingers long, fit for Apollo's Lute;
Her slipper such as Momus dare not mock;[4]
Her virtues all so great as make me mute:
  What other parts she hath I need not say,
  Whose face alone is cause of my decay.

1. parasitikh: parasitikh.
2. Nasus Aquilinus ex Persarum opinione maiestatem personae arguit.
3. Quale suo reciuit funere carmen Olor. Strozza. et vide Plin. de cantu Olarino lib. 10. nat. hist. cap. 23.
4. Vide Chiliad r. cent. 5 adag. 74. vbi. Erasm. ex Philostrati ad vxorem epistola mutuatur.

VIII.

Acteon for espying Diana as she bathed her naked, was transformed into a Hart, and soon after torn in pieces by his own hounds, as Ovid describeth at large lib. 3. *Metamorph.* And *Silius Italicus libr.* 12. *de bello Punico* glanceth at it in this manner.

Fama est, cum laceris Actaeon stebile membris
Supplicium lueret fpectatae in sonte Dianae,
Attonitum nouitate mala fugisse parentem
Per freta Aristeum, etc.

The Author alluding in all this Passion unto the fault of Actaeon, and to the hurt which he sustained, setteth down his own amorous infelicity; as Ovid did after his banishment, when in another sense he applied this fiction unto himself, being exiled (as it should seem) for having at unawares taken Caesar in some great fault: for thus he writeth.

Cur aliquid vidi, cur noxia lumina feci ? etc.
Inscius Actaeon vidit fine veste Dianam,
Praeda suit canibus nec minus ille suis.

Acteon lost in middle of his sport
Both shape and life, for looking but awry,
Diana was afraid he would report
What secrets he had seen in passing by:
  To tell but truth, the self same hurt have I
  By viewing her, for whom I daily die;
I leese my wonted shape, in that my mind
Doth suffer wrack upon the stony rock
Of her disdain, who contrary to kind
Doth bear a breast more hard than any stock;
  And former form of limbs is changed quite
  By cares in love, and want of due delight.
I leese my life in that each secret thought,
Which I conceive through wanton fond regard,
Doth make me say that life availeth nought
Where service cannot have a due reward:
  I dare not name the Nymph that works my smart,
  Though love hath grav'n her name within my heart.

IX.

Clytia (as Perottus witnesseth) was a glorious Nymph, and thereof had her name: for kleos in Greek signifieth glory: and therefore she aspired to be the love of Sol himself, who preferring Leucothoe before her, she was in short space over-gone with such extremity of care, that by compassion of the Gods she was transformed into a Marigold; which is significantly called Heliotropium, because even now after change of form she still observeth the rising and going down of her beloved the sun, as Ovid mentioneth,

Illa suum, quamuis radice tenetur,
Vertitur ad Solem, mutataque seruat amorem. Metam. lib. 4.

And by this it may easily be guessed, why in this passion the Author compareth himself with the Marigold and his love unto the Sun.

The Marigold so likes the lovely Sun,
That when he sets the other hides her face,
And when he gins his morning course to run,
She spreads abroad, and shows her greatest grace;
  So shuts or sprouts my joy, as doth this flower,
  When my She-sun doth either laugh or lower.
When she departs my sight, I die for pain,
In closing up my heart with cloudy care;
And yet when once I view her face again,
I straight revive, and joy my wonted fare:
  Therewith my heart oft says, when all is done,
  That heav'n and earth have not a brighter sun.
A jealous thought yet puts my mind in fear,
Lest Jove himself descending from his throne
Should take by stealth and place her in his sphere,
Or in some higher globe to rule alone:
  Which if he should, the heav'ns might boast their prey
  But I (alas) might curse that dismal day.

X.

The Author hath made two or three other passions upon this matter that is here contained, alluding to the loss of his sight and life since the time he first beheld her face, whose love hath thus bewitched him. But here he mentioneth the blindness of Tyresias to proceed of another cause than he doth in those his other Sonnets, And herein he leaneth not to the opinion of the greater sort of Poets, but unto some few, after whom Polytian hath written also, as followeth;

Baculum dat deinde petentem
Tyresiae magni, qui quondam Pallada nudam
Vidit, et hoc raptam penfauit munere lucem.
Suetus in offensos baculo duce tendere gressus
Nec deest ipse sibi, quin sacro instincta furore
Ora movet, tantique parat solatia damni.

Mine eyes die first, which last enjoyed life,[1]
Not hurt by bleared eyes, but hurt with light
Of such a blazing star as kindleth strife
Within my breast as well by day as night:
And yet no poisoned Cockatrice lurk'd there,
Her virtuous beams dissuade such foolish fear.
Besides, I live as yet; though blinded now
Like him, that saw Minerva's naked side,
And lost his sight (poor soul) not knowing how;
Or like to him, whom evil chance betide,
In straying far to light upon that place,
Where mid'st a fount he found Diana's grace.
But he alone, who Polyphemus hight,
True pattern was of me and all my woe,
Of all the rest that ever lost their sight:
For being blind, yet love possess'd him so,
That he each hour on ev'ry dale and hill
Sung songs of love to a Galatea still.[2]

1. Quod naturale esse, sit Plinius lib. ii. natur. his c. 36.
2. Galatea, daughter of Nereus, was a water nymph.

XI.

In this sonnet is covertly set forth how pleasant a passion the Author one day enjoyed, when by chance he overheard his mistress, whil'st she was singing privately by herself: And soon after into how sorrowful a dump, or sounden ecstasy he fell, when upon the first sight of him she abruptly finished her song and melody.

O Golden bird and Phoenix of our age,
Whose sweet records and more than earthly voice
By wondrous force did then my grief assuage
When nothing else could make my heart rejoice,
  Thy tunes (no doubt) had made a later end,
  If thou had'st known how much they stood my friend.
When silence drown'd the latter warbling note,
A sudden grief eclips'd my former joy,
My life itself in calling Charon's boat
Did sigh, and say that pleasure brought annoy;
  And blam'd mine ear for list'ning to the sound
  Of such a song, as had increas'd my wound.
My heavy heart rememb'ring what was past
Did sorrow more than any tongue can tell;
As did the damned souls that stood aghast,
When Orpheus with his wife return'd from hell:
  Yet who would think that Music which is sweet,
  In curing pains could cause delights to fleet?

XII.

The subject of the passion is all one with that which is next before it: but that the Author somewhat more highly here extolleth his lady's excellence, both for the singularity of her voice and her wonderful art in use and moderation of the same. But moreover, in this sonnet, the Author relateth how after the hearing of his mistress sing, his affection towards her by that means was more vehemently kindled than it had been at any time before.

I Marvel aye, why poets heretofore
Extoll'd Arion's harp or Mercury's,[1]
Although the one did bring a fish to shore,
And th' other as a sign adorn'd the skies.[2]
  If they with me had heard an Angel's voice,
  They would unsay themselves and praise my choice.
Not Philomela now deserves the prize,
Though sweetly she recount her cause of moan:
Nor Phoebus' art in musical device,
Although his lute and voice accord in one;
  Music herself, and all the Muses nine,
  For skill or voice their titles may resign.
O bitter sweet, or honey mix'd with gall,
My heart is hurt with over-much delight,
Mine ears well pleas'd with tunes, yet deaf withal:
Through music's help love hath increas'd his might;
  I stop mine ears as wise Ulysses bade,
  But all to late, now love hath made me mad.

1. Sic methymnaeo gauisus Arione Dolphin, Martial. lib. 8.
2. Consurgente freto cedit Lyra Cyllenaea Ruff. Fest.

XIII.

The Author descanteth on forward upon the late effect, which the song of his Mistress hath wrought in him, by augmenting the heat of his former love. And in this passion after he hath set down some miraculous good effects of Music, he falleth into question with himself, what should be the cause why the sweet melody of his Mistress should so much hurt him, contrary to the kind and nature of musical harmony.

AEsclepias did cure with trumpets' sound
Such men as first had lost their hearing quite:
And many such as in their drink lay drown'd
Damon reviv'd with tunes of grave delight:
  And Theophrast when ought his mind oppress'd,
  Us'd music's help to bring himself to rest:
With sound of harp Thales did make recure
Of such as lay with pestilence forlorn:
With Organ pipes Xenocrates made pure
Their wits, whose minds long Lunacy had worn:
  How comes it then, that music in my mind
  Enforceth cause of hurt against her kind?
For since I heard a secret heav'nly song,
Love hath so wrought by virtue of conceit,
That I shall pine upon supposed wrong
Unless she yield, that did me such deceit:
  O ears now deaf, O wits all drown'd in cares,
  O heart surpris'd with plagues at unawares.

XIIII.

The Author still pursuing his invention upon the song of his Mistress, in the last staff of this sonnet he falleth into this fiction: that whilest he greedily laid open his ears to the hearing of his Lady's voice, as one more than half in a doubt, that Apollo himself had been at hand, Love espying a time of advantage, transformed himself into the substance of air, and so deceitfully entered into him with his own great good will and desire, and now by main force still holdeth his possession.

Some that report great Alexander's life,
They say, that harmony so mov'd his mind,
That oft he rose from meat to warlike strife
At sound of Trump, or noise of battle kind,
  And then, that music's force of softer vein
  Caus'd him return from strokes to meat again.
And as for me, I think it nothing strange,
That music having birth from heav'ns above,
By divers tunes can make the mind to change:
For I myself in hearing my sweet Love,
  By virtue of her song both tasted grief,
  And such delight as yielded some relief.
When first I gan to give attentive ear,
Thinking Apollo's voice did haunt the place,
I little thought my Lady had been there:
But whilest mine ears lay open in this case,
  Transform'd to air Love entered with my will,
  And now perforce doth keep possession still.

XV.

Still he followeth on which further device upon the late Melody of his Mistress: and in this sonnet doth namely prefer her before Music herself, and all the three Graces; affirming if either he or else Apollo be ordained a judge, to give sentence of their deserts on either side, that then his Lady cannot fail to bear both prick and prize away.

Now Music hide thy face or blush for shame,
Since thou hast heard her skill and warbling voice,
Who far before thyself deserves thy name,
And for a Science should be had in choice:
  Or if thou still thy title wilt retain,
  Equal her song with help of all thy train.
But as I deem, it better were to yield
Thy place to her, to whom the prize belongs,
Then after strife to leese both fame and field.
For though rude Satyrs like Marsyas' songs,
  And Coridon esteem his oaten quill:
  Compare them with her voice, and both are ill.
Nay, which is more, bring forth the Graces three,
And each of them let sing her song apart,
And who doth best twill soon appear by me,
When she shall make reply which rules my heart:
  Or if you needs will make Apollo judge,
  So sure I am to win I need not grudge.

XVI.

In this passion the Author upon the late sweet song of his Mistress, maketh her his bird; and therewithal partly describeth her worthiness, and partly his own estate. The one part he showeth, by the color of her feathers, by her stately mind, and by that sovereignty which she hath over him: the other, by description of his delight in her company, and her strangeness, and drawing back from a due acceptance of his service.

My gentle bird, which sung so sweet of late,
Is not like those, that fly about by kind,
Her feathers are of gold, she wants a mate,
And knowing well her worth, is proud of mind:
  And whereas some do keep their birds in cage,
  My bird keeps me, and rules me as her page.
She feeds mine ear with tunes of rare delight,
Mine eye with loving looks, my heart with joy,
Wherehence I think my servitude but light,
Although in deed I suffer great annoy:
  And (sure) it is but reason, I suppose,
  He feel the prick, that seeks to pluck the Rose.
And who so mad, as would not with his will
Leese liberty and life to hear her sing,
Whose voice excels those harmonies that fill
Elysian fields, where grows eternal spring?
  If mighty Jove should hear what I have heard,
  She (sure) were his, and all my market marr'd.

XVII.

The Author not yet having forgotten the song of his mistress, maketh her in this passion a second Phoenix, though not of Arabia, and yet no less acceptable to Apollo, than is that bird of Arabia. And the chief causes why Sol should favor her, he accounteth to be these two, her excellent beauty, and her skill in music, of which two qualities Sol is well known to be an especial chief patron, and sometimes the only author or giver of the same.

If Poets have done well in times long past,
To gloze on trifling toys of little price:
Why should not I presume to fain as fast,
Espying forth a ground of good device?
  A Sacred Nymph is ground whereon I'll write,
  The fairest Nymph that ever yet saw light.
And since her song hath fill'd mine ears with joy,
Her virtues pleas'd my mind, her face mine eye,
I dare affirm what some will think a toy,
She Phoenix is, though not of Araby;
  And yet the plumes about her neck are bright,
  And Sol himself in her hath chief delight.[1]
You that will know why Sol affords her love,
Seek but the cause why Peacocks draw the place,
Where Juno sits; why Venus likes the Dove;
Or why the Owl befits Minerva's grace;
  Then if you grudge, that she to Sol belong,
  Mark but her face, and hear her skill in song.

1. Vide Plinium Natur. hist. lib. 10 cap. 2.

XVIII.

This sonnet is perfectly pathetical, and consisteth in two principal points: whereof the first containeth an accusation of Love for his hurtful effects and usual tyranny; the second part is a sudden recantation or excuse of the Author's evil words, by casting the same upon the neck of his beloved, as being the only cause of his late frenzy and blasphemous rage so lavishly poured forth in foul speeches.

Love is a sour delight; a sug'red grief;
A living death; an ever-dying life;
A breach of Reason's law; a secret thief;
A sea of tears; an ever-lasting strife;
  A bait for fools; a scourge of noble wits;
  A Deadly wound; a shot which ever hits.
Love is a blinded God; an angry boy;
A Labyrinth of doubts; an idle lust;
A slave to Beauty's will; a witless toy;
A ravening bird, a tyrant most unjust;
  A burning heat; a cold; a flatt'ring foe;
  A private hell; a very world of woe.
Yet mighty Love regard not what I say,
Which lie in trance bereft of all my wits,
But blame the light that leads me thus astray,
And makes my tongue blaspheme by frantic fits:
  Yet hurt her not, left I sustain the smart,
  Which am content to lodge her in my heart.

XIX.

The Author in this passion reproveth the usual description of love; which old Poets have so long time embraced; and proveth by probabilities that he neither is a child (as they say) not blind, nor winged like a bird, nor armed archer like with bow and arrows, neither frantic, nor wise, nor yet unclothed, nor (to conclude) any God at all. And yet when he hath said all he can to this end, he crieth out upon the secret nature and quality of Love, as being that, whereunto he can by no means attain, although he have spent a long and tedious course of time in his service

If Cupid were a child, as Poets feign,
How comes it then that Mars doth fear his might?
If blind; how chance so many to their pain,
Whom he hath hit, can witness of his sight?
  If he have wings to fly where thinks him best,
  How haps he lurketh still within my breast?
If bow and shafts should be his chiefest tools,
Why doth he set so many hearts on fire?
If he were mad, how could he further fools
To whet their wits, as place and time require?
  If wise, how could so many leese their wits,
  Or dote through love, and die in frantic fits?
If naked still he wander too and fro,
How doth not Sun or frost offend his skin?
If that a God he be, how falls it so,
That all wants end, which he doth once begin?
  O wondrous thing, that I, whom Love hath spent,
  Can scarcely know himself, or his intent.

XX.

In this passion the Author being joyful for a kiss, which he had received of his Love, compareth the same unto that kiss, which sometime Venus bestowed upon Aesculapius, for having taken a Bramble out of her foot, which pricked her through the hidden spiteful deceit of Diana, by whom it was laid in her way, as Strozza writeth. And he enlargeth his invention upon the French proverbial speech, which importeth thus much in effect, that three things proceed from the mouth which are to be had in high account: Breath, Speech, and Kissing; the first argueth a man's life; the second, his thought; the third and last, his love.

In time long past, when in Diana's chase
A bramble bush prick'd Venus in the foot,
Old AEsculapius help'd her heavy case
Before the hurt had taken any root:
  Wherehence although his beard were crisping hard
  She yielded him a kiss for his reward.
My luck was like to his this other day,
When she, whom I on earth do worship most,
For kissing me vouchsafed thus to say,
Take this for once, and make thereof no boast:
  Forthwith my heart gave sign of joy by skips,[1]
  As though our souls had join'd by joining lips.
And since that time I thought it not amiss
To judge which were the best of all these three;
Her breath, her speech, or that her dainty kiss,
And (sure) of all the kiss best liked me:
  For that was it, which did revive my heart
  Oppress'd and almost dead with daily smart.

1. Suquidem opinati sunt aliqui, in osculo fieri animarum combinationem.

XXI.

In the first staff of this passion the Author imitateth Petrarch, *Sonetto* 211.

Chi vuol veder quantunge puo Natura
El ciel tra noi, venga a mirar costeir, etc.

And the very like sense hath Seraphine in one of his *Strambotti*, where he beginneth thus,

Chi vuol ueder gran cose altiere e nuoue,
Venga a mirar costei, laquale adoro:
Dove gratia dal ciel continuo pioue. etc.

Who list to view dame Nature's cunning skill,
And see what heav'n hath added to the same,
Let him prepare with me to gaze his fill
On her apace, whose gifts exceed ye trump of fame:
  But let him come apace before she fly
  From hence, to fix her seat above the sky.
By Juno's gift she bears a stately grace,
Pallas hath placed skill amid'st her breast;
Venus herself doth dwell within her face;
Alas I faint to think of all the rest;
  And shall I tell wherewith I most have wars?
  With those her eyes, which are two heav'nly stars.
Their beams draw forth by great attractive power
My moistened heart, whose force is yet so small,
That shine they bright, or list they but to lower,
It scarcely dare behold such lights at all,
  But sobs, and sighs, and faith I am undone; [1]
  No bird but Jove's can look against the sun.

1. Vide Plin. nat. hist. lib. 10. cap. 3 et lib 29 cap. 6.qui de hac re mutuatur ex Aristotelis historia. Porro vide Seraphinum sonet. I. vbi de aquila suisque pullis per comparationem legantissime canit.

XXII.

The substance of this passion is taken out of Seraphine sonetto 127. which beginneth thus.

Quando nascesti amor? quando la terra
Se rinueste di verde e bel colore;
Di che susti creato? d'vn ardore,
Che cio lasciuo in se rinchiude e serera etc.

But the Author hath in this translation inverted the order of some verses of Seraphine. and added the two last of himself to make the rest to seem the more pathetical.

When wert thou born, sweet Love? Who was thy fire?
When Flora first adorn'd Dame Tellus' lap,
Then sprung I forth from Wanton hot desire:
Who was thy nurse to feed thee first with pap?
  Youth first with tender hand bound up my head,
  Then said, with Looks alone I should be fed;
What maids had she attendant on her side,
To play, to sing, to rock thee fast asleep?
Vain Niceness, Beauty Fair, and Pompous Pride;
By stealth when further age on thee did creep;
  Where did'st thou make thy chief abiding place?
  In Willing hearts, which were of gentle race;
What is't wherewith thou wagest wars with me?
Fear cold as ice, and Hope as hot as fire;
And cannot age or death make end of thee?
No, no, my dying life still makes retire;
  Why then, sweet Love, take pity on my pain,
  Which often die, and oft revive again.

XXIII.

The Author in this passion wisheth her were in like estate and condition with the Looking Glass of his mistress; by that means the oftener to be made happy with her favorable and fair aspect. And in the last staff he alludeth somewhat to the invention of Seraphine, where he useth these words, in writing upon the Glass of his beloved.

Che ho visto ogni qual vetro render foco
Quando e dal Sol percosso in qualche part,
E't Sol che in gliocchi toi dando in quel loco
Douria per reflexion tutta infiammarte etc.

Thou Glass, wherein that Sun delights to see
Her own aspect, whose beams have dried my heart,
Would God I might possess like state with thee,
And joy some ease to quail my bitter smart:
  Thou gazest on her face, and she on thine;
  I see not hers, nor she will look on mine.
Once having look'd her fill, she turns thee fro,
And leaves thee, though amaz'd, yet well content;
But careless of my cares, will I or no,
Still dwells within my breast with tears besprent;
  And yet my heart to her is such a thrall,
  That she driv'n out, my life departs withal.
But thou deceitful Glass (I fear) with guile
Hast wrought my woes to shield thyself from ill,
Short forth her beams which were in thee erewhile,
And burnt my tender breast against my will:
  For Crystal from itself reflects the Sun
  And fires his coat, which knows not how tis done.

XXIIII.

Seraphine in his *Strambotti* hath many pretty inventions concerning the Looking-glass of his Mistress: wherehence many particulars of this passion are cunningly borrowed, part being out of one place, and part out of another. And in the latter end is placed this fiction by the Author, that Cupid shooting his arrow from out the fair eyes of his Mistress, did so wound him with love and desire that now he is past all recure by any physic, and therefore is fain to use the old verse,

Hei mini quod nullus amor est medicabilis herbis.

Thou glass, wherein my Dame hath such delight,
As when she braves, then most on thee to gaze,
I marvel how her beams that are so bright
Do never cause thy brittle sides to craze:
  Thou should'st by reason melt or easily break
  To feel such force, thy substance being weak.
For when she first with seeming stately grace
Bestow'd on me a loving sweet regard,
The beams, which then proceeded from her face
Were such, as for the same I found no ward,
  But needs perforce I must become content
  To melt in mind till all my wits were spent.
And therewithal Cupid played his part,
He shot a shaft throughout her crystal eyes,
Wherewith he cleft in twain my yielding heart:
And this is cause my panting heart still cries,
  I break, I melt, help heav'ns in my behove,
  No herb doth grow whose virtue cureth love.

XXV.

It is to be considered in reading this Passion, how in some answers, the accent or pointing of the words is altered, and therewithal how the Author walking in the woods, and bewailing his inward passion of Love, is contraried by the replies of Echo: whose meaning yet is not so much to gainsay him, as to express her own miserable estate in daily consuming away for the love of her beloved Narcissus; whose unkindness Ovid describeth at large, together with the extreme love of Echo.(1)

Author. In all this world I think none loves but I.
  Echo. None loves but I.
Author. Thou foolish tattling guest, in this thou tell'st a lie.
  Echo. Thou tell'st a lie.
Author. Why? *Love* himself he lodgeth in my breast.
  Echo. He lodgeth in my breast.
Author. I pine for grief; and yet I want relief.
  Echo. I want relief.
Author. No star more fair than she whom I adore.
  Echo. Than he, whom I adore.[2]
Author. Herehence I burn still more and more.
  Echo. I burn still more and more,
Author. *Love*, let my heart return.
  Echo. My heart, return.
Author. Is then the *Saint*, for whom thou makest moan,
  And whom I love, but one?
  Echo. I love but one.
Author. O heav'ns, is there in love no end of ills?
  Echo. In love no end of ills.
Author. Thou prattling voice.
  Dwell'st thou in th' air, or but in hollow hills?
  Echo. In hollow hills.
Author. Cease of to vaunt thy choice.
  Echo. Cease off to vaunt thy choice.
Author. I would reply, but here for love I die.
  Echo. For love I die.

1. Lib. 3. Metamorph.
2. S. Liquescens immutat sensum.

XXVI.

Here the Author as a man overtaken with some deep melancholy, compareth himself unto the Nightingale, and conferreth his unhappy estate (for that by no means his Mistress will pity him) with her nightly complaints: to whose harmony all those that give attentive ear, they conceive more delight in the musical variety of her notes, than they take just compassion upon her distressed heaviness.

When May is in his prime, and youthful spring
Doth clothe the tree with leaves, and ground with flowers,
And time of year reviveth ev'ry thing;
And lovely Nature smiles, and nothing lowers;
  Then Philomela most doth strain her breast
  With night-complaints, and fits in little rest.
This Bird's estate I may compare with mine,
To whom fond love doth work such wrongs by day,
That in the night my heart must needs repine,
And storm with sighs to ease me as I may;
  Whil'st others are becalm'd, or lie them still.
  Or sail secure with tide and wind at will.
And as all those, which hear this Bird complain,
Conceive in all her tunes a sweet delight,
Without remorse, or pitying her pain:
So she, for whom I wail both day and night,
  Doth sport herself in hearing my complaint;
  A just reward for serving such a Saint.

XXVII.

In the first six verses of this Passion, the Author hath imitated perfectly six verses in an Ode of Ronsard, which beginneth thus:

Celui qui n'ayme est malheureux, . . En son 2. liure
Et malheureux est l'amoureux, ... du Bocage.
Mais la misere, etc.?

And in the last staff of this Passion also he cometh very near to the sense which Ronsard useth in another place, where he writeth to his Mistress in this manner:

En vens tu baiser Pluton
La bas, apres che Caron . . . . En ses meslanges.
T'aura mise en sa nacesse?

Unhappy is the wight that's void of Love,[1]
And yet unhappy he, whom Love torments,
But greatest grief that man if forc'd to prove,
Whose haughty Love not for his love relents,
  But hoising up her sail of proud disdain,
  For service done makes no return of gain.
By this all you, which know my tickle state,
May give deserved blame to whom I serve,
And say, that Love hath misery to mate,
Since labor breeds but loss, and lets me starve:
  For I am he which lives a lasting thrall
  To her, whose heart affords no grace at all.
She hopes (perchance) to live and flourish still,
Or else, when Charon's boat hath felt her peace,
By loving looks to conquer Pluto's will;
But all in vain: t'is not Proserpin's ease:
  She never will permit that any one
  Shall joy his Love, but she herself alone.

1. Hii tres versus a Ronsardo describuntur ex Anacreonte Graeco.

XXVIII.

In this Passion the Author doth very busily imitate and augment a certain Ode of Ronsard, which he writeth unto his Mistress; he beginneth as followeth,

Plusieurs de leurs cors denues
Se sont veuz en diverse terre
Miraculeusement mues, ... Au luire des les
L'vn en Serpent, et l'autre en Pierre, . . meslanges.
L'vn en Fleur, latre en Arbrisseau
L'vn en Loup etc.?

Many have liv'd in countries far and nigh,
Whose hearts by Love once quite consum'd away,
Strangely their shapes were changed by and by,
One to a Flow'r, another to a Bay,
  One to a Stream, whose course yet maketh moan,
  One to a Dove, another to a Stone,
But hark my Dear; if wishing could prevail,
I would become a Crystal Mirror aye,
Wherein thou might'st behold what thing I ail:
Or else I would be chang'd into a Fly,
  To taste thy cup, and being daily guest
  At board and bed, to kiss thee mid'st thy rest;
Or I would be Perfume for thee to burn,
That with my loss I might but please thy smell;
Or be some sacred Spring, to serve thy turn,
By bathing that wherein my heart doth dwell;
  But woe is me, my wishing is but vain,
  Since fate bids Love to work my endless pain.

XXIX.

The Author in this Sonnet in a large manner setteth forth the surpassing worthiness of his Lady, reporting her beauty and form to be so singular that neither Appelles can perfectly draw her portrait; nor Praxiteles truly frame her image and likeness in any kind of metal. And the like unableness he awardeth unto Virgil and Homer the two Paragons of Poetry, if they should but once endeavor to praise her. And the like insufficiency he sayeth would be found in Tully himself, if he should endeavor to commend her. And then finally he excuseth his own bold hardiness showed in praising her, upon the forcible extremity which he abideth in Love, and the earnest desire which he hath to please.

Such is the Saint whom I on earth adore,
As never age shall know when this is past,
Nor ever yet hath like been seen before;
Apelles if he liv'd would stand aghast
  With colors to set down her comely fare,[1]
  Who far excels though Venus were in place.
Praxiteles might likewise stand in doubt
In metal to express her form aright,
Whose praise for shape is blown the world throughout:
Nor Virgil could so good a verse indite
  As only would suffice to tell her name;
  Nor Homer with his Muse express her fame;
Tully whose speech was bold in ev'ry cause,
If he were here to praise the Saint I serve,
The number of her gifts would make him pause,
And fear to speak how well she doth deserve.
  Why then am I thus bold that have no skill?
  Enforc'd by Love I show my zealous will.

1. Here he alludeth unto the portrait of Venus which Apelles drew: as Ovid doth. lib. 3. de art. aman. Si Venerem Cous nunquam pinxisset Appelles.

XXX.

In the first part of this Passion the Author proveth that he abideth more unrest and hurt for his beloved than ever did Leander for his Hero: of which two paramours the mutual fervency in Love is most excellently set forth by Musaeus the Greek Poet. In the second part he compareth himself with Pyrarmus and Haemon, king Creon's Son of Thebes, which were both so true-hearted lovers that through Love they suffered untimely death, as Ovid *Metam*. lib. 4. writeth at large of the one, And the Greek Tragedian Sophocles in *Antig*. of the other. In the last, in making comparison of his pains in Love to the pains of Orpheus descending to hell for his Eurydice, he alludeth to those two verses in Strozza.

Tartara, Cumba, Charon, Pluto, rota, Cerberus, angues,
Cocytes, Phlegeton, Styx, lapis, urna, fitis.

What though Leander swam in darksome night,
Through troubled Hellespont for Hero's sake;
And lost his life by loss of Sestus' light?
The like or more myself do undertake,
  When ev'ry hour along the ling'ring year,
  My joy is drown'd, and hope blown out with fear.
And what though Priam spent his vital breath
For Thisbe's sake? or Haemon chose to die
To follow his Antigone by death?
In harder case and worser plight am I,
  Which love as they, but live in dying still,
  And fain would die, but cannot have my will.
We read that Orpheus with his Harp of gold,
For his Erydice went down to hell:
The toil is more, by that time all be told,
Which I endure for her, whose heart is fell;
  The Stygian Cur, the Wheel, the Stone, the Fire.
  And Furies all are plac'd in my desire.

XXXI.

There needeth no annotation at all before this Passion, it is of itself so plain and easily conveyed. Yet the unlearned may have this help given them by the way to know what Galaxia is, or Pactolus, which perchance they have not read of often in our vulgar Rhymes. Galaxia (to omit both the Etymology and what the Philosophers do write thereof) is a white way or milky Circle in the heavens, which Ovid mentioneth in this manner.

Est via sublimis coelo manifesta sereno, ... Metamorph.
Lactea nomen habet, candore notabilis ipso. . . . . lib. I.

And Cicero thus in *somnio Scipionis; Erat autem is splendidissimo candore inter flammas circulus elucens, quem vos (ut a Graijs accepistis) orbem lacteum nuncupatis.*

Pactolus is a river in Lydia, which hath golden sands under it, as Tibullus witnesseth in this verse,

Nec me regna juvant, nec Lydias auriser amnis. . Tibul. lib. 3

Who can recount the virtues of my dear,
Or say how far her fame hath taken flight,
That can not tell how many stars appear
In part of heav'n, which Galaxia height,
  Or number all the motes in Phoebus rays,
  Or golden sands, whereon Pactolus plays?
And yet my hurts enforce me to confess,
In crystal breast she shrouds a bloody heart,
Which heart in time will make her merits less,
Unless betimes she cure my deadly smart:
  For now my life is double dying still,
  And she defam'd by suff'rance of such ill;
And till the time she helps me as she may,
Let no man undertake to tell my toil,
But only such, as can distinctly say,
What Monsters Nilus breeds, or Affricke soil:
  For if he do, his labor is but lost,
  Whil'st I both fry and freeze twixt flame and frost.

XXXII.

Here the Author by feigning a troublesome dream, expresseth a full Passion of Love. And howsoever some will conster of this kind of invention, it is evident that the like hath been usual amongst those that have excelled in the sweetest vein of Poetry. And (to let the rest go,) it may please him that is curious to find some precedent hereof, to visit but the works of Hercules Strozza,(1) who in his *Somnium* hath written so exquisitely, that the Dream will quite his travail, that shall peruse it with due attention.

In Thetis' lap, while Titan took his rest,
I slumb'ring lay within my restless bed,
Till Morpheus us'd a falsed sorry jest,
Presenting her, by whom I still am led:
  For then I thought she came to end my woe,
  But when I wak'd (alas) t'was nothing so.
Embracing air instead of my delight,
I blamed Love as author of the guile,
Who with a second step clos'd up my sight,
And said (methought) that I must bide a while.
  Ixion's pains, whose arms did oft embrace
  False darken'd clouds, instead of Juno's grace,
When I had lain and slumber'd thus a while,
Ruing the doleful doom that Love assign'd,
A woman Saint, which bare an Angel's face,
Bad me awake and ease my troubled mind:
  With that I wak'd, forgetting what was past,
  And saw t'was Hope, which helped thus at last.

1. Eroticon lib. 2.

XXXIII.

In this Sonnet the Author is of opinion that his Mistress (by the fatal appointment of destiny) was from the beginning reserved to live in these times, and to be the only governess and subject of his thoughts: whereas: if either she had been borne when Paris was to give sentence upon Ida for bestowing the Golden Apple; she had (as he supposeth) been preferred before Juno, Pallas and Venus, and moreover supplied that place in the love of king Priam's son, which Helen of Greece obtained: or if she had then lived when Bacchus took Ariadne to wife, she had been conveyed in her stead, unto that place in heav'n where now the Crown of Ariadne called *Corona Gnosia*[1] doth shine continually, being beautified with great variety of lightsome stars.

When Priam's son in mid'st of Ida plain
Gave one the prize, and other two the foil,
If she for whom I still abide in pain
Had lived then within the Trojan soil,
  No doubt but hers had been the golden ball,
  Helen had scaped rape, and Troy his fall.
Or if my Dame had then enjoyed life
When Bacchus fought for Ariadne's love,
No doubt but she had only been his wife,
And flown from hence to sit with Gods above:
  For she exceeds his choice of Crete so far
  As Phoebus doth excel a twinkling star.
But from the first all fates have thus assign'd,
That she should live in these our latter days,
I think to bear a sway within my mind
And feed my thoughts with friendly sweet delays;
  If so it be, let me attend my chance,
  And fortune pipe when I begin to dance.[2]

1. Cuius ortum et occasum memorat Plinius nat. hist. lib. 18. c. 28. et. c. 31.
2. Assai ben balla a chi Fortuna suona.

XXXIIII.

The Author in this Sonnet very highly commendeth the most rare excellencies of his mistress, avouching her to have no equal. And he imitateth the second Sonnet, *Nelle rime di messer Agnolo Fiorenzuola the Florentine*, whose beginning is all one with that here; and this it is:

Deh le mie belle done et amorose,
Ditemi il ver per vostra cortesia,
Non e chiara tra voi la donna mia,
Come e'l Sol chiar tro tutte l' altre cose?

Ye stately Dames, whose beauties far excel,
Of courtesy confess at my request,
Doth not my Love amongst you bear the bell,
As Phoebus golden rays obscures the rest
  Of Planet Stars, and dimmeth ev'ry light
  That shines in heav'n or earth by day or night?
Take wistly heed in viewing her sweet face,
Where nature hath express'd what ere she could
Either for beauty's blaze or comely grace:
Since when to prize her work she break the mold,
  So that who seeks to find her Equal out,
  Intends a thing will nere be brought about.
Therefore sweet Ladies all vouchsafe with me
To follow her desert and my desire,
By praising her unto the ninth degree,
For honor by due right is virtue's hire,
  And Envy's mouth must say when all is done,
  No Bird but one is sacred to the sun.

XXXV.

In this Passion the Author, as being blinded with Love, first compareth himself with Tyresias the old Soothsayer of Thebes, whom Juno deprived of sight; but Jove rewarded him with the spirit of prophecy. Then he alludeth unto Acteon: And lastly he showeth why he is in worse case than those, which by viewing Medusa's head were turned into stones, leesing both life and light at once; and so concludeth that old accursed Oedipus of all other best befitteth him for a companion.

When first mine eyes were blinded with Desire,
They had new seen a Second Sun, whose face,
Though clear as beaten snow, yet kindled fire
Within my breast, and moult my heart apace:
  Thus learned I by proof what others write,
  That Sun and fire, and snow offend the sight.
O ten-times-happy blinded Theban wight,
Whose loss of sight did make him half divine,
Where I (alas) have lost both life and light,
Like him, whose horns did plague his heedless eyen;
  And yet was he in better case than I,
  Which neither live, nor can obtain to die.
All Perseus' foes that saw Medusa's head,
By leesing shape and sense were quit from thrall;
But I feel pains, though blind and double-dead,
And was myself efficient cause of all:
  Wherefore, of all that ere did cease to see
  Old Oedipus were meetest mate for me.[1]

1. Vide Sophocl. and Seneca in tragedijs suis de Oedipi miserijs.

XXXVI.

Here the Author misliketh of his wearisome estate in love, for that he neither obtaineth any favor at the hands of his Mistress for his good thought or speech, nor by his loving looks, or presents, nor by his humility in writing, or long sufferance in servitude. And herehence he blameth her over-hardness of heart, and the froward constellation of his own nativity: and therewithal abandoning all further desire of life, hath in request untimely death, as the only end of his infelicity.

Each thought I think is friend to her I Love;
I still in speech use course of gentle words;
My loving looks are such as ought to move;
My gifts as great as mine estate affords;
  My letters tell in what a case I stand,
  Though full of blots through fault of trembling hand;
I duly dance attendance as I may,
With hope to please, and fear to make offense,
With sov'reignty to her I grant for aye;
And where she hurts yet make I no defense;
Sobs are the song wherein I take delight;
  And show'rs of tears do daily dim my sight.
  And yet all this doth make but small avail,
Her heart is hard and never will relent;
No time, no place, no prayer can prevail,
The heav'ns themselves disfavor mine intent:
  Why should I then desire a longer life,
  To weave therein a web of endless strife?

XXXVII.

The Author in this passion doth by manner of secret comparison prefer his beloved before all other women whatsoever: and persuadeth upon the examples of all sorts of Goddess (whom love hath overtaken at one time or other) that the worthiness of his Mistress being well considered, his own fondness in love must of force be in itself excusable.

If Jove himself be subject unto Love
And range the woods to find a mortal prey:
If Neptune from the seas himself remove,
And seek on sands with earthly wights to play:
  Then may I love my peerless choice by right,
  Who far excels each other mortal wight.
If Pluto could by love be drawn from hell,
To yield himself a silly Virgin's thrall:
If Phoebus could vouchsafe on earth to dwell,
To win a rustic maid unto his call:
  Then, how much more should I adore the sight
  Of her, in whom the heav'ns themselves delight?
If country Pan might follow Nymphs in chase,
And yet through love remain devoid of blame:
If Satyrs were excus'd for seeking grace
To joy the fruits of any mortal Dame:
  Then, why should I once doubt to love her still,
  On whom ne Gods nor men can gaze their fill?

XXXVIII.

In the first staff of this Passion the Author expresseth how fondly his friends over-trouble him, by questioning with him touching his love, or accidents thereof. In the two last verses of the second staff he imitateth those verses of Sophocles: *In Trachinijs.* which may be thus Englished,

That man, which champion like will strive with Love
And combat hand-to-hand, hath little wit:
For as he list he rules the Gods above.

And in the last, he setteth down his mind fully bent to persist constantly in the love and service of his Lady: like to that which Stephanus Forcatulus (an excellent Civilian, and one of the best Poets of France for these many years) wrote unto his beloved *Clytia*:

Quin noctu pluuium citius mirabimur arcum,
Solque domo Hesperidum mane propinquus erit,
Quam capiat lepidae me foeda obliuio nymphae, etc.?

Some ask me, when and how my love begun;
Some, where it lies, and what effects it hath;
Some, who she is, by whom I am undone;
Some, what I mean to tread so lewd a path;
  I answer all alike by answ'ring nought,
  But, blest is he whom Cupid never caught:
And yet I could, if sorrow would permit.
Tell when and how I fix'd my fancy first,
And for whose sake I lost both will and wit,
And chose the path wherein I live accurst:
  But such-like deeds would breed a double sore,
  „ For love gainsaid grows madder than before,
But note herewith that so my thoughts are bound
To her in whom my liberty lies thrall,
That if she would vouchsafe to salve my wound,
Yet force of this my love should never fall,
  Till Phoebus use to rise from out the West,
  And towards night seek lodging in the East.

XXXIX.

The second part of this Passion is borrowed from out the fifth Sonnet in Petrarch part I, whose words are these,

Piu volte gia per dir le labbra apersi:
Poi rimase la voce in mezz'l petto:
Ma qual suon poria mai salir tansalto?
Piu volte incominciai di feriuer versi,
Ma la penna, e la mano, e lo' intelletto
Rimaser vinto net primier aaaalto.

When first these eyes beheld with great delight
The Phoenix of this world, or second Sun,
Her beams or plumes bewitched all my sight,
And love increas'd the hurt that was begun:
  Since when my grief is grown so much the more,
  Because I find no way to cure the sore,
I have attempted oft to make complaint,
And with some doleful words to tell my grief,
But through my fearful heart my voice doth faint,
And makes me mute where I should crave relief:
  Another while I think to write my pain,
  But straight my hand lays down the pen again.
Sometimes my mind with hopes of doubtful cares
Conjoin'd with fawning heaps is sore oppress'd,
And sometimes sudden joy at unawares
Doth move too much, and so doth hurt my breast;
  What man doth live in more extremes than these,
  Where death doth seem a life, and pains do please?

XL.

The sense contained in this Sonnet will seem strange to such as never have acquainted themselves with Love and his Laws, because of the contrarieties mentioned therein. But to such, as Love at any time hath had under his banner, all and every part of it will appear to be a familiar truth. It is almost word for word taken out of Petrarch, (where he beginneth,

Pace mon truouo, e mon ho da far guerra; . . *Parte prima*
E temo, espero, etc.?) . . . . Sonet. 105.

All, except three verses, which this Author hath necessarily added for perfecting the number, which he hath determined to use in every one of these his Passions.

I Joy not peace, where yet no war is found;
I fear, and hope; I burn, yet freeze withal;
I mount to heav'n, yet lie but on the ground;
I compass nought, and yet I compass all;
  I live her bond, which neither is my foe,
  Nor friend; nor holds me fast, nor lets me go;
Love will not that I live, nor lets me die;
Nor locks me fast, nor suffers me to scape;
I want both eyes and tongue, yet see and cry;
I wish for death, yet after help I gape;
  I hate myself, but love another wight;
  And feed on grief, in lieu of sweet delight;
At self same time I both lament and joy;
I still am pleas'd, and yet displeased still;
Love sometimes seems a God, sometimes a Boy;
Sometimes I sink, sometimes I swim at will;
  Twixt death and life, small difference I make;
  All this, dear Dame, befalls me for thy sake.

XLI.

This Passion is framed upon a somewhat tedious or too much affected continuation of that figure in Rhetoric, which of the Greeks is called *paltlsgia* or *anadiplosis*, of the Latins Reduplicatio; whereof Susenbrotus (if I well remember me) allegeth this example out of Virgil,

Sequitur pulcherrimus ustur, . . .Aeneid. 10.
Auftur equo fidens.

O Happy men that find no lack in Love
I Love, and lack what most I do desire;
My deep desire no reason can remove;
All reason shuns my breast, that's set on fire;
  And so the fire maintains both force and flame,
  That force availeth not against the same;
One only help can slake this burning heat,
Which burning heat proceedeth from her face,
Whose face by looks bewitched my conceit,
Through which conceit I live in woeful case;
  O woeful case, which hath no end of woe,
  Till woes have end by favor of my foe;
And yet my foe maintaineth such a War,
As all her War is nothing else but Peace;
But such a Peace as breedeth secret jar,
Which jar no wit, nor force, nor time can cease;
  Yet cease despair: for time by wit, or force,
  May force my friendly foe to take remorse.

XLII.

In this Passion the Author under color of telling his dream doth very cunningly and lively praise his Mistress, so far forth as not only to prefer her before Helen of Greece for excellence of beauty, but also before how many soever are now living in this our age. The dream of itself is so plainly and effectually set down (albeit in few words) that it need no further annotation to explain it.

This latter night amidst my troubled rest
A Dismal Dream my fearful heart appall'd,
Whereof the sum was this: Love made a Feast.
To which all Neighbor, Saints and Gods were call'd:
  The cheer was more than mortal men can think,
  And mirth grew on, by taking in their drink.
Then Jove amidst his cups for service done
Gan thus to jest with Ganymede his boy;
I fain would find for thee my pretty Son
A fairer Wife than Paris brought to Troy:
  Why, sir, quoth he, if Phoebus stand my friend,
  Who knows the world, this gyre will soon have end.
Then Jove replied that Phoebus should not choose
But do his best to find the fairest face;
And she once found should neither will nor choose
But yield herself, and change her dwelling-place;
  Alas, how much was then my heart affright
  Which bade me wake and watch my fair delight?

XLIII.

The sense or matter of this Passion is taken out of Seraphine in his *Strambotti*, who writeth thus,

Se Salamandra in fiamma viue, e in suoco,
Non me stupisce quel che fa natura,
Ma costei che e di giaccio, e io di suoco,
E in mezo del mio cuor vuie sicura;
Chi la defende in cosi ardente suoco,
Che douendo fguagliar diventa dura?
Solo Amor di Natura aspro adversario,
Che a suo dispetto unisce ogni contrario.

The Salamander lives in fire and flame,
And yet but wonder small in Nature's work:
By stranger force love wins away her fame,
As causing cold in midst of heart to lurk.
  Who list of these my pains to take the view,
  Will soon confess that what I say is true.
For one as cold as hardest frozen ice,
Is fixed fast, and lodgeth in my breast;
Whom reason can remove by no device,
Nor any force can cause to let me rest:
  And yet I still so swim in hot desire,
  That more I burn than either flame or fire.
How strange is this? Can contraries so gree,
That Ice in flame will neither waste nor melt,
But still increase, and harder grow to be,
Than erst before? All this myself have felt.
  For Love, Dame Nature's foe, without remorse,
  Thus coupleth contraries in me by force.

XLIIII.

In this Passion the Author misliketh one while his estate, and by and by after liketh of the same again, upon hope and likelihood of amendment, and throughout the whole Sonnet he sayeth his Mistress to be a Second Sun, and by expressing his private infelicity, in either always melting away with Love, or growing stiff through Death approaching near him by reason of daily cares, he maketh allusion unto the diver effects of the Sun, which maketh the day much harder, and the wax softer, than it was before.

That Second Sun, whose beams have dimm'd my sight,
So scorched hath my heart and senses all,
That clogg'd with cares and void of all delight,
I only seek, and sue to be her thrall;
  Yet so this heat increaseth day by day,
  That more and more it hast'neth my decay.
Sometimes I melt, as if my limbs were wax,
Sometimes grow stiff, as if they were of clay;
Thrice happy he whom Love doth never vex,
For any Second Sun doth melt away:
  Nay cursed I blaspheme the fairest Light
  That ever yet was seen by day or night.
Perchance her parching heats will once repair
My heart again, and make me all anew:
The Phoenix so revives amidst the air
By virtue of that Sun which all men view:
  The virtue of my Sun exceeds the sky,
  By her I shall revive, though first I die.

XLVI.

Here the Author bewaileth the extremity of his estate growing daily to be more troublesome than before, and all through the hard heart of his beloved: whom he therefore aptly compareth unto a stony rock, which nothing can move or waste away but long continuance of time. And hereupon, after having long strived with himself and his passions, he is quietly resolved to have patience, and so long to persevere in the still-hoping mind of a true lover, till by long continuance of time Love be induced to stand his friend.

All ye that love compare your pains with mine,
Which void of hope continue still her thrall,
Whose heart is hard, and never will assign
A ransom-day, nor once will bow at all,
  Much like the stony rock, whose harden'd side
  Will scarcely wear with course of time or tide.
And yet, since time can wear each thing away,
I will enforce myself to live content,
Till so my thoughts have fed upon delay,
That Reason rule the roast and love relent;
  O vain attempt in striving with Despair,
  I build nought else but castles in the air.
For why: the Sun may sooner shine by night,
And twinkling stars give glimsing sparks by day:
Then I can cease to serve my Sweet delight,
Whom neither force nor time can drive away:
  Therefore in hope that love will stand my friend
  I thus conclude, Each thing but love hath end.

XLVII.

This Passion containeth a relation throughout from line to line; as, from every line of the first staff as it standeth in order, unto every line of the second staff; and from the second staff unto the third. The oftener it is read of him that is no great clerk, the more pleasure he shall have in it. And this poesy a scholar set down over this Sonnet, when he had well considered of it: *Tam cafu, quam art et industria.* The two first lines are an imitation of Seraphine, *Sonnetto* 103.

Col tempo et Villanello all giogo mena
El Tor si fiero, e si crudo animale,
Col tempo el Falcon s'vsa a menar l'ale
E ritornare a te chiamando a pena.

In time the Bull is brought to wear the yoke;
In time all haggard Hawks will stoop the Lures;
In time small wedge will cleave the sturdiest Oak;
In time the Marble wears with weakest showers:
  More fierce is my sweet love, more hard withal,
  Than Beast, or Bird, than Tree or Stony wall.
No yoke prevails, she will not yield to might;
No Lure will cause her stoop, she bears full gorge;
No wedge of woes make print, she recks no right;
No shower of tears can move, she thinks I forge:
  Help therefore Heav'nly Boy, come pierce her breast
  With that same shaft which robs me of my rest.
So let her feel thy force, that she relent;
So keep her low, that she vouchsafe a pray;
So frame her will to right, that pride be spent;
So forge, that I may speed without delay;
  Which if thou do, I'll swear and sing with joy,
  That Love no longer is a blinded Boy.

XLVIII.

This Passion containeth two principal points. In the first are placed two similitudes; in both which the Author expresseth his own willfulness in love. In the second, he compareth the beautiful eyes of his Mistress unto the eyes of the Basilisk, which killeth a man with his only sight being a far off; whereof Lucan lib. 9. sayeth thus,

Sibilaque effundens cunctas terrentia pestes,
Ante venena nocens, late sibi submouet omne
Vulgus, et in vacua regnat Basiliscus arena.
And Mantuan in like manner. *Natus in ardenti Libyae Basiliscus arena,*
Vulnerat aspectu, luminibusque necat.

Like as the silly Bird amid'st the night,
When Birders beat the bush, and shake his nest,
He flutt'ring forth straight flies unto the light,
As if it were the day new-sprung from East,
Where so his willful wings consume away,
That needs he must become the Birder's prey:
Or, as the Fly, when candles are alight,
Still plays about the flame until he burn:
Even so my heart hath seen a heav'nly sight,
Wherehence again it hardly can return:
The beams thereof contain such wond'rous flame,
That Jove himself would burn to see the same.
I mean a Virgin's face, whose beauty rare,
Much like the Basilisk in Lybia soil,
With only sight is cause of all my care,
And loads my yielding heart with endless toil;
Yet needs I must confess she hath more grace
Than all the Nymphs that haunt Diana's chase.

XLIX.

The Author in this Song bewrayeth his daily Passions in love to be so troublesome, that to avoid the flames thereof, he gladly and fain would yield himself to die, were it not that he feareth a further inconvenience would then arise. For he doubteth lest those flames, wherein his soul continually burneth, shall make Charon afraid to grant him passage over the Lake of Styx, by reason, his old withered boat is apt to take fire.

So great a Light hath set my mind on fire,
That flesh and bone consume with secret flame,
Each vein dries up, wit yields to deep desire;
I scarce (alas) dare say, for very shame,
  How fain my soul an interchange would make
  Twixt this her present State and Limbo lake;
And yet she dreads, lest when she parts from hence,
Her Heats be such that Charon will retire,
And let her pass for prayer, nor for pence, [1]
For fear his with'red boat be set on fire;
  So dang'rous are the flames of Mighty Love
  In Styx itself, in earth, or heav'n above.
Wherefore dear Dame vouchsafe to rue my case,
And salve the sore which thou thyself hast made:
My Heats first grew by gazing on thy face,
Whose lights were such that I could find no shade:
  And thou my weary Soul bend all thy force,
  By Plaints and Tears to move her to remorse.

1. Naulum intelligit, de quo Iuuenal: Miserum est post omnia perderee naulum.

L.

In this Passion is effectually set down in how strange a case he liveth that is in love, and in how contrary an estate to all other men, which are at defiance with the like folly. And this the Author expresseth here in his own person: therewithal calling upon Love, to stand his friend; or if he fail, upon death to cut off his wearisome life.

While others feed, my fancy makes me fast;
While others live secure, I fear mischance;
I dread no force, where other stand aghast;
I follow suit where Fortune leads the Dance,
  Who like a mumming mate so throws the Dice,
  That Reason leesing all, Love wins the price;
Which Love by force so worketh in my breast,
That needs perforce I must incline my will
To die in dreams while others live in rest,
And live in woes while others feel none ill.
  O gentle Death, let here my days have end,
  Or mighty Love, so use me as thy friend.
Mine eyes are worn with tears, my wits with woe,
My color dried with cares, my heart with pains,
My will bewitch'd, my limbs consumed so,
That scarcely blood or vital breath remains:
  While others joy or sleep, I wail and wake:
  All this (Dear Dame) I suffer for thy sake.

LI.

Tityus was the son of Jupiter, and for attempting to dishonest Latona, was slain by Apollo. Since which time the Poets feign that for punishment he lieth in hell, miserably tormented with a ravening Vulture, which feedeth upon his bowels continually: and they as they are consumed, still miraculously grow up again, to breed his endless misery, as the Poet witnesseth,

Quid dicam Tityum, cuius sub vulnere faeuo Claud. in
Viscera nascuntur grauibus certantia paenis? Gigantomachia.

The Author compareth his passions with the pains of this Tityus, and imitateth Seneca writing to like effect,

Vulture relicto transuolet Tityo serus,
Meumque paena semper addrescat iecur.

If Tityus wretched wight beheld my pains,
He would confess his wounds to be but small,
A Vulture worse than his tears all my veins,
Yet never lets me die, nor live at all:
  Would Gods a while I might possess his place,
  To judge of both, which were in better case.
The Hell is dark, wherein he suff'reth smart,
And wants not some Compartners of his grief:
I live in Light, and see what hurts my heart,
But want some mourning mates for my relief;
  His Pain is just reward, his crimes were such:
  My greatest fault is this, I love too much.
Why then, since too much love can breed offense,
Thou dang'rous Bird, the root of my desire,
Go perch elsewhere, remove thyself from hence;
I freeze like Ice, and burn like flaming fire:
  Yet stay good Bird: for if thou soar away,
  Twixt Frost and Flame my days will soon decay.

LII.

Here the Author after some dolorous discourse of his unhappiness, and rehearsal of some particular hurts which he sustaineth in the pursuit of his love: first questioneth with his Lady of his desert; and then, as having made a sufficient proof of his innocence, persuadeth her to pity him whom she herself hath hurt. Moreover, it is to be noted that the first letters of all the verses in this Passion being joined together as they stand, do contain this poesy agreeable to his meaning, *Amor me pungit et vrit.*

A A World of woes doth reign within my breast,
m My pensive thoughts are cov'red all with care,
o Of all that sing the Swan doth please me best.
r Restraint of joys exiles my wonted fare,
M   Mad-mooded Love usurping Reason's place
e   Extremity doth over-rule the case.
P Pain drieth up my veins and vital blood,
u Unless the Saint I serve give help in time:
n None else, but she alone, can do me good.
g Grant then, ye Gods, that first she may not climb
i   Immortal heav'ns, to live with Saints above,
t   Then she vouchsafe to yield me love for love
E Examine well the time of my distress
t Thou dainty Dame, for whom I pine away,
V Unguilty though, as needs thou must confess,
r Rememb'ring but the cause of my decay;
i   In viewing thy sweet face arose my grief,
t   Therefore in time vouchsafe me some relief

LIII.

The two first parts of this Sonnet, are an imitation of certain Greek verses of Theocritus; which verses as they are translated by many good Poets of later days, so most aptly and plainly by C. Urcinus Velius in his *Epigrams*; he beginneth thus,

Nuper apis furem pupugit violenter Amorem
Ipsum ex alueolis clam mella favosque legentem,
Cui summos manuum digitos confixit, at ille
Indoluit, lafae tumuerunt vulnere palmae:
Planxit humum, et faltu trepidans pulsavit, et ipsi
Oftendens Veneri, casum narrauit acerbum, etc.

Where tender Love had laid him down to sleep,
A little Bee so stung his finger's end,
That burning ache enforced him to weep
And call for Phoebus' Son to stand his friend,[1]
  To whom he cried, I muse so small a thing
  Can prick thus deep with such a little Sting.
Why so, sweet Boy, quoth Venus sitting by?
Thyself is young, thy arrows are but small
And yet thy shot makes hardest hearts to cry?
To Phoebus' Sun she turned therewithal,
  And prayed him show his skill to cure the sore,
  Whose like her Boy had never felt before.
Then he with Herbs recured soon the wound,
Which being done, he threw the Herbs away,
Whose force, through touching Love, in self-same ground,
By hapless hap did breed my heart's decay:
  For there they fell, where long my heart had li'n
  To wait for Love, and what he should assign.

1. AEsculapius.

LIIII.

In this Passion the Author boasteth, how sound a pleasure he lately enjoyed in the company of his Beloved, by pleasing effectually all his five senses exterior, and that through the only benefit of her friendly presence, and extraordinary favor towards him. And in many choice particulars of this Sonnet, he imitateth here and there a verse of Ronsard's, in a certain *Elegy* to Janet peintre du Roy: which beginneth thus,

Pein moi, Ianet, pein moi ie te supplie
Dans ce tableau les beautes de m'amie
De la facon, etc.

What happy hour was that I lately past
With her, in whom I fed my senses all?
With one sure sealed kiss I pleas'd my taste;
Mine ears with words, which seemed Musical;
  My smelling with her breath, like Civet sweet;
  My touch in place where modesty thought meet,
But shall I say, what objects held mine eye?
Her curled Locks of Gold, like Tagus' sands;
Her Forehead smooth and white as Ivory,
Where Glory, State and Bashfulness held hands;
  Her Eyes, one making Peace, the other Wars;
  By Venus one, the other rul'd by Mars;
Her Eagle's Nose; her Scarlet Cheeks half white;
Her Teeth of Orient Pearl; her gracious smile;
Her dimpled Chin; her Breast as clear as light;
Her Hand like hers who Tithon did beguile.[1]
  For worldly joys who might compare with me,
  While thus I fed each sense in his degree?

1. Aurora.

LV.

The whole invention of all this Passion is deducted out of Seraphine, *Sonnet* 63, whose verses if you read, you will judge this Author's imitation the more praiseworthy; these they are,

Come alma asai bramosa e poco accorta
Che mai visto havea amor fe mon depinto,
Disposi un ai cercar fuo Laberinto,
Vedere el monstro, e tanta gente morta.
Ma quel fil deragion che chi per scorta
Del qual su tutto el ceco loco cinto
Subito, ahime, su da lui rotto e vinto,
Talche mai piu trouar seppi la porta.

My heedless heart which Love yet never knew,
But as he was describ'd with Painter's hand,
One day amongst the rest would needs go view
The Labyrinth of Love, with all his band.
To see the Minotaur his ugly face,
And such as there lay slain within the place.
But soon my guiding thread by Reason spun,
Wherewith I pass'd along his darksome cave,
Was broke (alas) by him, and overrun,
And I perforce became his captive slave:
Since when as yet I never found the way
To leave that maze wherein so many stray.
Yet thou on whom mine eyes have gaz'd so long
May'st, if thou wilt, play Ariadne's part,
And by a second Thread revenge the wrong,
Which through deceit hath hurt my guiltless heart;
Vouchsafe in time to save and set me free,
Which seek and serve none other Saint but thee.

LVI.

The first Staff of this Passion is much like unto that invention of Seraphine in his *Strambotti*, where he sayeth,

Morte: che voui? te bramo: Eccomi appresso;
Prendemi: a che? che manchi el mio dolore;
Non posso: ohime, non puoi? non per adesso;
Perche? pero che in te non regna il core, etc.

The second Staff somewhat imitateth another of his *Strambotti* in the same leaf; it beginneth thus,

Amor, amor: chi e quel che chiama tanto?
Un tuo seruo fidel; uon ti consfco; etc.

The Author in the last Staff, returneth to entreat Death anew, to end his days

Come gentle Death; who calls? One that's oppress'd:
What is thy will? That thou abridge my woe,
By cutting off my life; cease thy request,
I cannot kill thee yet: alas, why so?
  Thou want'st thy Heart. Who stole the same away?
  Love, whom thou serv'st, entreat him sigh thou may.
Come, come, come Love: who calleth me so oft?
Thy Vassal true, whom thou should'st know by right.
What makes thy cry so faint? My voice is soft,
And almost spent by wailing day and night.
  Why then, what's thy request? That thou restore
  To me my Heart, and steal the same no more.
And thou, O Death, when I possess my Heart,
Dispatch me then at once: why so?
By promise thou art bound to end my smart.
Why, if thy Heart return, then what's thy woe?
  That brought from cold, it never will desire
  To rest with me, which am more hot than fire.

LVII.

Here the Author cheerfully comforting himself, rebuketh all those his friends, or others whatsoever, which pity his estate in Love: and groundeth his invention, for the most part, upon the old Latin Proverb, *Confuetudo eft altera natura.* Which Proverb he confirmeth by two examples; the one, of him, that being born far North seldom catcheth cold; the other of the Negro, which being born under a hot climate, is never smothered with over-much heat.

All ye, that grieve to think my death so near,
Take pity on yourselves, whose thought is blind;
Can there be Day, unless some Light appear?
Can fire be cold, which yieldeth heat by kind?
  If Love were past, my life would soon decay,
  Love bids me hope, and hope is all my stay.
And you that see in what estate I stand,
Now hot, now cold, and yet am living still,
Persuade yourselves, Love hath a mighty hand,
And custom frames what pleaseth best her will.
  A ling'ring use of Love hath taught my breast
  To harbor strife, and yet to live in rest.
The man that dwells far North hath seldom harm
With blast of winter's wind or nipping frost:
The Negro seldom feels himself too warm
If he abide within his native coast;[1]
  So, Love in me a Second Nature is,
  And custom makes me think my Woes are Bliss.

1. For both experience teacheth and Philosophical reason approveth, than an Ethiopian may easily in Spain be smothered with the heat of the country though Spain be more temperate than Ethiopia is.

LVIII.

Aetna, called in times past *Inesia*, as Volaterranus witnesseth, is a hollow hill in Sicilia, whose top burneth continually, the fire being maintained with a vein of brimstone, and other such like Minerals, which are within the said Mountain. Which notwithstanding, the bottom of the hill is very pleasant, as well for the abundance of sweet fruits and flowers, as for the number of fresh springs and fountains. The Poets feign that when Jupiter had with his thunderbolts beaten down the Giants of the earth, which rebelled against heaven, he did forthwith cover and oppress them all with the weight of this hill Aetna. These things being well considered, together with the verse of Horace:

(*Deus immortalis haberi De art Poetica*
Dum cupit Empedocles, ardentem frigidus AEtnam Insiluit.)

It may easily appear why the Author in this passion compareth his heart unto the hill.

There is a monstrous hill in Sicil soil,
Where works that limping God, which Vulcan hight,
And rebel Giants lurk, whom Jove did foil,
When gainst the heav'ns they durst presume to fight;
  The top thereof breaths out a burning flame,
  And Flora sits at bottom of the same.
My swelling heart is such another hill,
Wherein a blinded God bears all the sway,
And rebel thoughts resisting reason's skill
Are bound by will from starting thence away;
  The top thereof doth smoke with scalding smart,
  And seldom joys obtain the lowest part.
Yet learn herewith the diff'rence of the twain:
Empedocles consum'd with Aetnae's fire
When godhead there he fought, but all in vain:
But this my heart, all flaming with desire,
  Embraceth in itself an Angel's face,
  Which beareth rule as Goddess of the place.

LIX.

The Author in this Passion accuseth his own eyes, as the principal or only cause of his amorous infelicity; wherein his heart is so oppressed continually with evils, which are contrary in themselves, that reason can bear no sway in the cause. Therefore in the end, he instantly entreateth his Lady of her speedy favor and good-will, alleging what hurt may grow through her longer delay.

That thing wherein mine eyes have most delight,
Is greatest cause my heart doth suffer pain:
Such is the hurt that comes by wanton sight;
Which reason strives to vanquish all in vain;
  This only sense, more quick than all the rest,
  Hath kindled holy fire within my breast.
And so my mourning heart is parching dry
With sending sighs abroad and keeping care,
What needs it must consume if long it lie
In place, where such a flame doth make repair:
  This flame is Love, whom none may well entreat,
  But only she, for whom I suffer heat.
Then peerless Dame, the ground of all my grief,
Vouchsafe to cure the cause of my complaint:
No favor else but thine can yield relief.
But help in time, before I further faint,
  For Danger grows by ling'ring till the last,
  And physic hath no help when life is past.

LX.

The Author groundeth this Passion upon three points. In the first, he showeth how he witting and willfully followeth his own hurt, with such like words as Medea sometime used,

Video meliora, proboque, *Ovid Metam*
Deteriora sequor, etc. *lib.* 7.

In the second, he excuseth his fault upon the main force and tyranny of Love, being the only governor of his will. And lastly, he humbly entreateth his Lady for the restitution of his wonted liberty: desiring her not to exact more of him than his ability of body or mind can well sustain, according to the old verse,
Pelle magis rabida nihil est de Vulpe petendum.

Was ever man, whose Love was like to mine?
I follow still the cause of my distress,
My Heart foreseeing hurt, doth yet incline
To seek the same, and thinks the harm the less.
In doing thus, you ask me what I ail:
Against main force what reason can prevail?
Love is the Lord and Signor of my will,
How shall I then dispose of any deed?
By forced Bond, he holds my freedom still,
He dulls each sense, and makes my heart to bleed.
Thou Sacred Nymph, whose virtue wanteth stain,
Agree with Love and set me free again.
Of this my weary Life no day shall fall,
Wherein my pen shall once thy praise forget:
No Night with sleep shall close mine eyes at all,
Before I make recount of such a debt;
Then force me not to more than well I may,
Besides his Skin, the Fox hath nought to pay.

LXI.

The invention of this Passion is borrowed, for the most part from Seraphine *Son. 125.* Which beginneth,

S'el gran tormento i fier fulmini accesi
Perduti havessi, e li fuoi strali Amore,
In'ho tanti trassitti in meggio el core,
Che fel da me li potriano esser resi;
E se de gli ampli mari in terra stefi
Fusse privo Neptuno, io spando fore
Lagryme tante, che con piu liquore
Potrebbe nuoui mari haver ripresi; etc.

If Love had lost his shafts, and Jove down threw
His thund'ring bolts and spent his forked fire,
They only might recov'red be anew
From out my Heart cross-wounded with desire;
  Or if Debate by Mars were lost a space,
  It might be found within the self-same place;
If Neptune's waves were all dried up and gone,
My weeping eyes so many tears distill,
That greater Seas might grow by them alone;
Or if no flame were yet remaining still
  In Vulcan's forge, he might from out my breast
  Make choice of such as should befit him best.
If Aeole were depriv'd of all his charge,[1]
Yet soon could I restore his winds again,
By sobbing sighs, which forth I blow at large,
To move her mind that pleasures in my pain;
  What man but I could thus incline his will
  To live in Love, which hath no end of ill?

1. (Graves) Eldest son of Hellen (ancestor of the Greeks), who became guardian of the winds.

LXII.

That the vulgar sort may the better understand this Passion, I will briefly touch those whom the Author nameth herein, being all damned souls (as the Poets feign) and destinate unto sundry punishments. Tantalus having his lips still at the brink of the river Eridanus, yet dieth for thirst. Ixion is tied unto a wheel; which turneth incessantly. A vulture feedeth upon the bowels of Tityus, which grow up again ever as they are devoured. Sisyphus rolleth a great round stone up a steep hill, which being once at the top presently falleth down amain. Belides are fifty sisters whose continual task is to fill a bottomless tub full of water, by lading in their pitchers full at once.[1]

In that I thirst for such a Goddess' grace
As wants remorse, like Tantalus I die;
My state is equal to Ixion's case,
Whose rented limbs are turn'd eternally,
  In that my tossing toils can have no end,
  Nor time, nor place, nor chance will stand my friend.
In that my heart consuming never dies,
I feel with Tityus an equal pain,
On whom an ever-feeding Vulture lies;
In that I rise through hope, and fall again
  By fear, like Sisyphus I labor still
  To turle a rolling stone against the hill,
In that I make my vows to her alone,
Whose ears are deaf and will retain no sound,
With Belides my state is all but one,
Which fill a tub whose bottom is not sound.
  A wondrous thing, that Love should make the wound,
  Wherein a second Hell may thus be found.

1. (Graves) The 50 daughters of Danaus were forced to marry the sons of their father's Danaus' enemy, his twin brother Agenor. 49 of the Danaids murdered their new husbands and were condemned to the endless task of carrying water in jars perforated like sieves.

LXIII.

Love hath two arrows, as Conradus Celtis witnesseth in these two verses:

Per matris aftrum, et per fera specula, Odarum. lib. I
Quae bina sert saeuus Cupido, etc.

The one is made of lead, the other of gold, and either of them different in quality from the other. The Author therefore feigneth in this Passion, that when Cupid had stroken him with that of lead, soon after pitying his painful estate, he thought good to strike his beloved with the other. But her breast was so hard that the shaft rebounding back again, wounded Love himself at unawares. Wherehence fell out these three inconveniences; first, that Love himself became her thrall, whom he should have conquered; then, that she became proud, where she should have been friendly; and lastly, that the Author by this means despaireth to have any recure of his unquiet life, and therefore desireth a speedy death, as alluding to those sententious verses of Sophocles' *Electra* which may be thus Englished paraphrastically,

What can it him avail to live a while,
Whom, of all others, evils are betide?

Love hath two shafts, the one of beaten gold,
By stroke whereof a sweet effect is wrought:
The other is of lumpish leaden mold,
And worketh none effect, but what is nought:
  Within my breast the latter of the twain
  Breeds fear, fear thought, and thought a lasting pain.
One day amongst the rest sweet Love began
To pity mine estate, and thought it best
To pierce my Dear with gold, that she might scan
My case aright, and turn my toils to rest:
  But from her breast more hard than hardest flint
  His shaft flew back, and in himself made print.
And this is cause that Love doth stoop her lure,
Whose heart he thought to conquer for my sake;
That she is proud; and I without recure:
Which triple hurt doth cause my hope to quake:
  Hope lost breeds grief, grief pain, and pain disease,
  Disease brings death, which death will only please

LXIIII.

This Passion is of like frame and fashion with that which was before under the number of XLI, whetherto I refer the Reader. But touching the sense or substance of this Passion, it is evident that herein the Author, by laying open the long continued grievesomness of his misery in Love, seeketh to move his Mistress to some compassion.

My humble suit hath set my mind on pride,
Which pride is cause thou hast me in disdain.
By which disdain my wounds are made so wide,
That wideness of my wounds augments my pain,
  Which Pain is cause, by force of secret jars,
  That I sustain a brunt of private Wars.
But cease, dear Dame, to kindle further strife,
Let Strifes have end, and Peace enjoy their place;
If Peace take place, Pity may save my life,
For Pity should be shown to such as trace
  Most dang'rous ways, and tread their steps awry,
  Or live my woes: and such a one am I.
Therefore, My Dear Delight, regard my Love,
Whom Love doth force to follow Fond Desire,
Which Fond Desire no counsel can remove;
For what can counsel do to quench the fire
  That fires my heart through fancy's wanton will?
  Fancy by kind with Reason striveth still.

LXV.

In the first and second part of this passion, the Author proveth by examples, or rather by manner of argument, *A maiori ad minus*, that he may with good reason yield himself to the empire of Love, whom the gods themselves obey; as Jupiter in heaven, Neptune in the seas, and Pluto in hell. In the last staff he imitateth certain Italian verses of M. Girolamo Parabosco; which are as followeth.

Occhi tuoi, anzi stelle alme, et fatali, Selva Seconda.
Oue ha prescritto il ciel mio mal, mio been:
Mie lagrime, e sospir, mio riso. e canto;
Mia spene, mio timor; mio feco e giaccio;
Mia noia, mio piacer; mia vito e morte.

Who knoweth not how often Venus' son
Hath forced Jupiter to leave his seat?
Or else, how often Neptune he hath won
From seas to sands, to play some wanton feat?
  Or how he hath constrain'd the Lord of Styx
  To come on earth, to practice loving tricks?
If heav'n, if seas, if hell must needs obey,
And all therein be subject unto Love,
What shall it then avail if I gainsay
And to my double hurt his pow'r do prove?
  No, no, I yield myself, as is but meet:
  For hitherto with sour he yields me sweet.
From out my Mistress eyes, two lightsome stars,
He destinates estate of double kind,
My tears, my smiling *cheer*, my peace, my wars;
My sighs, my songs; my fear, my hoping mind;
  My fire, my frost; my joy, my sorrow's gall;
  My curse, my praise; my death, but life with all.

LXVI.

This Latin passion is borrowed from Petrarch *Sonetto 133.* which beginneth.

Hor, ch'l ciel, e la terra e'l vento tace,
E le fere, e gli angelli il fonno affrena,
Notte 'l carro stellato in giro mena,
E nel suo letto il mar fenz'onda giace; etc.

Wherein he imitated Virgil, speaking of Dido, thus.

Nox erat, et tacitum carpebant fesa soporem Corpora etc.

And this Author presumeth, upon the pains he hath taken, in faithfully translating it, to place it amongst these his own passions, for a sign of his great sufferance in love.

LXVII.

A man singular for his learning, and magistrate of no small accompt, upon slight survey of this book of passions, either for the liking he had to the Author, or for his own private pleasure, or for some good he conceived of the work, vouchsafed with his own hand to set down certain poesies concerning the same: amongst which this was one, *Love* hath no leaden heels. Whereat the Author glanceth throughout all this Sonnet; which he purposely compiled at the press, in remembrance of his worshipful friend, and in honor of his golden poesy.

When Cupid is content to keep the skies,
He never takes delight in standing still,
But to and fro, and ev'rywhere he flies,
And ev'ry God subdueth at his will.
  As if his bow were like to Fortune's wheel,
  Himself like her, having no leaden heel.
When other whiles he passeth Lemnos Ile,
Unhappy boy he gibes the Clubfoot Smith,[1]
Who threatens him, and bids him stay a while,
But laughing out he leaves him he forthwith,
  And makes himself companion with the Wind
  To show his heels are of no leaden kind.
But in myself I have too true a proof:
For when he first espied my ranging Heart,
He Falcon-like came sousing from aloof
His swiftly falling stroke encreas'd my smart:
  As yet my Heart the violence it feels,
  Which makes me say, *Love* hath no leaden heels.

1. Vulcan.

LXVIII.

The Author hath wrought this passion out of certain verses of Stephanus Forcatulus, which are these.

Cor mihi punxit amor, sed punxit praepete telo;
figitur hoc tum plus, cum magis excutio, etc.
Carpere dictamum Cretaea nil iuvet Ida;
quo vellunt cerui spicula fixa leves.
Telephus haec eadem fatalia vulnera sensit,
fanare ut tantum, qui facit illa, queat.

And thereas the Author in the end of this passion, alludeth to the wounds of Telephus, he is to be understood of that Telephus, the Son of Hercules, of whose wound, being made and healed by Achilles only, Ovid writeth thus.

Vulnus Achillaeo quod quondam fecerat hosti, De remed.
Vulneris auxilium Pelias hasta tulit lib. 1.
And Propertius in like manner lib. 2.
Mysus et Haemonia iuuenis qui cuspide vulnus
Senserat, hac ipsa cuspide sensit opem.

Suidas mentioneth another Telephus, an excellent Grammarian of Pergamus.

In secret seat and center of my heart,
Unwares to me, not once suspecting ill,
Blind Cupid's hand hath fix'd a deadly dart,
Whereat how ere I pluck, it sticketh still,
  And works effect like those of Arab soil,
  Whose heads are dipp'd in poison stead of oil.
If't were like those, wherewith in Ida plain
The Cretan hunter wounds the chased deer,
I could with Dictame draw it out again,
And cure me so, that scar should scarce appear.
  Or if Aldices shaft did make me bleed,[1]
  Machaon's art would stand me in some stead.
But being as it is, I must compare
With fatal wounds of Telephus alone,
And say that he, whose hand hath wrought my care,
Must either cure my fatal wound, or none:

Help therefore, gentle Love, to ease my heart,
Whose pains increase, till thou withdraw thy dart.

1. He alludeth to the wound of Philoctetes. (Graves) Machaon, a son of Asclepius, tended the wounded during the siege of Troy Philoctetus had been bitten by a poisonous snake during the gathering of the Greeks, or hit by one of Hercules poisoned arrows. His painful and noxious wound was long-lasting but not fatal.

LXIX.

In the first staff of this Passion, The Author, as one more than half drooping with despair, sorrowfully recounteth some particular causes of his unhappiness in Love. In the residue he entreateth a better aspect of the Planets, to the end that either his life may be inclined to a more happy course, or his death be hastened, to end all his misery at once.

My joys are done, my comfort quite dismay'd,
My weary wits bewitch'd with wanton will,
My will by Fancy's heedless fault betray'd,
Whose eyes on Beauty's face are fixed still,
  And whose conceit Folly hath clouded so,
  That Love concludes, *my heart must live in woe.*
But change aspect, ye angry stars above,
And pow'rs divine restore my liberty,
Or grant that soon I may enjoy my Love,
Before my life incur more misery:
  For now so hot is each assault I feel
  As would dissolve a heart more hard than steel.
Or if you needs must work my deadly smart,
Perform your charge by hasting on my death
In sight of her, whose eyes enthrall my heart:
Both life and death to her I do bequeath,
  In hope at last, she will vouchsafe to say,
  I rue his death, whose life I made away.

LXX.

In this passion the Author somewhat afar off imitateth an Ode in *Gervasius Sepinus* written to Cupid, where he beginneth thus:

Quid tenelle puer, Pharetra ubinam est? Erotopaegnicon.
Ubi arcus referens acuta Lunoe lib. I.
Bina cornua? vbi flagrans Ameris
fax? ubi igneus ille arcus, in quo
De ipsis Caelicolis, virisque victis
Vinctisque ante ingum aurcus triumphas?
Haud posent tua summa numina unam,
Vnam vincere Virginem tenellam?
Qui fortes animos pudica Elisoe
Fortioribus irrigans venenis
Vicisti: etc.

Cupid, where is thy golden quiver now?
Where is thy sturdy Bow? And where the fire
Which made ere this the Gods themselves to bow?
Shall she alone, which forceth my Desire,
  Report or think thy Godhead is so small,
  That she through pride can scape from being thrall?
Whilom thou overcam'st the stately mind
Of chaste Eusa queen of Carthage land,[1]
And did'st constrain Pasiphae gainst her kind,
And broughtest Europa fair to Creta sand,
  Quite through the swelling Seas, to pleasure Jove,
  Whose heav'nly heart was touch'd with mortal love.
Thus wert thou wont to show thy force and flight,
By conq'ring those that were of highest race,
Where now it seems thou changest thy delight.
Permitting still, to thy no small disgrace,
  A virgin to despise thyself, and me,
  Whose heart is hers, wheree'er my body be.

1. Possibly the Queen of Elphame, whose rites were related to those of the lotus-eaters (see Graves).

LXXI.

The Author writeth this Sonnet unto his very friend, in excuse of his late change of study, manners, and delights, all happening through the default of Love. And here by examples he proveth unto him (calling him by the name of Titus, as if himself were Gusippus) that Love not only worketh alteration in the minds of men, but also in the very Gods themselves; and that so far forth, as first to draw from their Celestial seats and functions, and then to ensnare them with the unseemly desire of mortal creatures, a Passion ill-befitting the majesty of their Godheads.

Alas, dear Titus mine, my ancient friend,
What makes thee muse at this my present plight,
To see my wonted joys enjoy their end
And how my Muse hath lost her old delight?
This is the least effect of Cupid's dart,
To *change* the mind by wounding of the heart.
Alcides fell in love as I have done,
And laid aside both club and Lion's skin;
Achilles too when he fair Brises won,
To fall from wars to wooing did begin.
Nay, if thou list, survey the heav'ns above,
And see how Gods themselves are chang'd by Love.
Jove steals from skies to lie by Leda's side;
Arcas descends for fair Aglaurus' sake,
And Sol, so soon as Daphne is espied,
To follow her his Chariot doth forsake:
No marvel then, although I change my mind,
Which am in love with one of heav'nly kind.

LXXII.

In this Sonnet The Author seemeth to specify that his Beloved maketh her abode in this our beautiful and fair City of London; situate upon the side of the Thames, called in Latin Thamesis. And therefore, whil'st he feigneth that Thamesis is honorably to be conveyed hence by all the Gods towards the Palace of old Nereus, he seemeth to grow into some jealousy of his mistress, whose beauty if it were as well known to them as it is to him, it would (as he sayeth) both deserve more to be honored by them, and please Triton much better, than Thamesis, although she be the fairest daughter of old Oceanus.

Oceanus not long ago decreed
To wed his dearest daughter Thamesis
To Triton, Neptune's son, and that with speed:
When Neptune saw the match was not amiss,
  He prayed the Gods from highest to the least,
  With him to celebrate the Nuptial feast.
Love did descend with all his heav'nly train,
And came for Thamesis to London side,
In whose conduct each one employ'd his pain
To reverence the state of such a Bride:
  But whil'st I saw her led to Nereus' Hall,
  My jealous heart began to throb withal.
I doubted aye, lest any of that crew,
In fetching Thamesis, should see my Love,
Whose ticing face is of more lively hue,
Than any Saint's in earth or heav'n above:
  Besides, I fear'd that Triton would desire
  My Love, and let his Thamesis retire.

LXXIII.

Here the Author, by feigning a quarrel betwixt Love and his Heart, under a shadow expresseth the tyranny of the one and the misery of the other: to stir up a just hatred of the one's injustice, and cause the due compassion of the other's unhappiness. But as he accuseth Love for his readiness to hurt where he may; so he not excuseth his Heart for desiring a fair imprisonment when he needed not: thereby specifying in Love a willful malice, in his Heart a heedless folly.

I Rue to think upon the dismal day
When Cupid first proclaimed open war
Against my Heart; which fled without delay,
But when he thought from Love to be most far,
  The winged boy prevented him by flight,
  And led him captive-like from all delight.
The time of triumph being overpast,
He scarcely knew where to bestow the spoil,
Till through my heedless Heart's desire, at last,
He lock'd him up in Tower of endless toil.
  Within her breast, whose hardened will doth vex
  Her silly guest softer than liquid wax.
This prison at the first did please him well,
And seem'd to be some earthly Paradise,
Where now (alas) Experience doth tell,
That Beauty's bates can make the simple wise,
  And bids him blame the bird, that willingly
  Chooseth a golden cage for liberty.

LXXIIII.

The Author in this passion, upon a reason secret unto himself, extolleth his Mistress under the name of a Spring. First he preferreth the same before the sacred fount of Diana, which (as Ovid witnesseth 3. *Metam*) was in the valley Gargaphy adjoining to Thebes: then, before Tagus the famous river in Spain, whose sands are intermixed with store of gold, as may be gathered by those two verses in *Martial* lib. 8.

Non illi fatis est turbato fordidus auro
Hermus, et Hesperio qui fonat orbe Tagus.

And lastly, before Hippocrene, a fountain of Boetia, now called the well of the Muses, and feigned by the Poets to have had his source or beginning from the heel of Pegasus the winged horse.

Although the drops which chang'd Acteon's shape,
Were half divine, and from a sacred fount;
Though after Tagus' sands the world do gape;
And Hippocrene stand in high account:
  Yet there's a Spring whose virtue doth excel
  Diana's fount, Tagus, and Pegas' well.
That happy hour wherein I found it first,
And sat me down adjoining to the brink,
My foe itself, surpris'd with unknow'n thirst,
Did wish it lawful were thereof to drink;
  But all in vain: for Love did will me stay
  And wait a while in hope of such a prey.
This is that Spring quoth he, where Nectar flows,
Whose liquor is of price in heav'ns above;
This is the Spring wherein sweet Venus shows,
By secret bait how Beauty forceth Love.
  Why then, quoth I, dear Love how shall I mend,
  Or quench my thirst unless thou stand my friend?

LXXV.

In this passion the Author borroweth from certain Latin verses of his own, made long ago upon the love abuses of Jupiter in a certain piece of work written in the commendation of womenkind; which he hath not yet wholly perfected to the print. Some of the verses may be thus cited to the explaining of this passion, although but lamely.

Accipe ut ignaram candentis imagine Tauri
Luserit Europam ficta etc.
Quam nimio Semelen fuerit complexus amore, etc.
Qualis et Asterien aquilinis pressrit alis:
Quoque dolo Laedam sicto sub olore fefellit.
Adde quod Antiopam Satyri sub imagine etc.
Et suit Amphytrio, cum te Tirynthia etc.
Parrhasiam fictae pharetra Vultuque Dianae,
Mnemosynen pastor; serpens Deoida lusit, etc.

Ovid writeth somewhat in like manner. *Metam*. lib. 6.

Not she, whom Jove transported into Crete;
Nor Semele, to whom he vow'd in haste;
Nor she whose flanks he fill'd with feigned heat;
Nor whom with Eagles' wings he oft embrac'd;
  Nor Danae, beguil'd by golden rape;
  Nor she for whom he took Diana's shape;
Nor fair Antiopa, whose fruitful love
He gained Satyr-like; nor she whose Son
To wanton Hebe was conjoin'd above;
Nor sweet Mnemosyne, whose love he won
  In shepherd's weed; no such are like the Saint
  Whose eyes enforce my feeble heart to faint.
And Jove himself may storm, if so he please,
To hear me thus compare my Love with his:
No forked fire, nor thunder can disease
This heart of mine, where stronger torment is:
  But O how this surpasseth all the rest,
  That she, which hurts me most, I love her best.

LXXVI.

In this Sonnet the Author being, as it were, in half a madding mood, faileth at variance with Love himself, and blasphemeth his godhead, as one that can make a greater wound than afterwards he himself can recure. And the chief cause that he setteth down why he is no longer to hope for help at Loves hand, is this, because he himself could not remedy the hurt which he sustained by the love of fair Psyches.[1]

Thou foolish God the Author of my grief,
If Psyche's beams could set thy heart on fire,
How can I hope, of thee to have relief,
Whose mind with mine doth suffer like desire?
  Henceforth my heart shall sacrifice elsewhere
  To such a Saint as higher port doth bear.
And such a Saint is she whom I adore,
As foils thy force and makes thee stand aloof;
None else but she can salve my festered sore;
And she alone will serve in my behoof:
  Then blinded boy, go pack thee hence away,
  And thou Sweet Soul, give ear to what I say.
And yet what shall I say? Strange is my case,
In mid'st of frost to burn, and freeze in flame:
Would Gods I never had beheld thy face,
Or else, that once I might possess the same:
  Or else that chance would make me free again,
  Whose hand help'd Love to bring me to this pain.

1. Vide Apul.

LXXVII.

The chief contents of the Passion are taken out of Seraphine *Sonnet*, 132.

Col tempo passa gli anni, i mefi, e l'hore,
Col tempo le richeze, imperio, e regno,
Col tempo fama, honor, fortezza, e ingegno,
Co

But this Author inverteth the order which Seraphine useth, sometimes for his rhyme's sake, but for the most part upon some other more allowable consideration.

TIme wasteth years, and month's, and hours:
Time doth consume fame, honor, wit and strength:
Time kills the greenest Herbs and sweetest flowers:
Time wears out youth and beauty's looks at length:
  Time doth convey to ground both foe and friend,
  And each thing else but Love, which hath no end.
Time maketh ev'ry tree to die and rot:
Time turneth oft our pleasures into pain:
Time causeth wars and wrongs to be forgot:
Time clears the sky, which first hung full of rain:
  Time makes an end of all human desire,
  But only this, which sets my heart on fire.
Time turneth into naught each Princely state:
Time brings a flood from new-resolved snow:
Time calms the Sea where tempest was of late:
Time eats what ere the Moon can see below:
  And yet no time prevails in my behove,
  Nor any time can make me cease to love.

LXXVIII.

This Passion concerneth the low'ring of his Mistress and herein for the most part the Author imitateth *Agnola firenzuola*; who upon the like subject writeth as followeth,

O belle done, prendam pietade
Di me pur hor'in talpa trafformato
D'huom, che pur dianza ordiua mirar fiso
Come Aquila il sol chiar in paradiso.
Cosi va'l mondo, e cosi spesso accade
A chi si fida inamoroso stato, etc.

What scowling clouds have overcast the sky,
That these mine eyes cannot, as wont they were,
Behold their second Sun intentively?
Some strange Eclipse is happ'ned as I fear,
  Whereby my Sun is either barr'd of light,
  Or I myself have lost my seeing quite.
Most likely so, since Love himself is blind,
And Venus too (perhaps) will have it so,
That Lovers wanting sight shall follow kind.
O then, fair Dames, bewail my present woe,
  Which thus am made a mole, and blindfold run
   Where Eagle-like I late beheld the Sun.
But out, alas, such guerdon is assign'd
To all that love and follow Cupid's car:
He tires their limbs and doth bewitch their mind,
And makes within themselves a lasting war.
  Reason with much ado doth teach me this,
  Though yet I cannot mend what is amiss.

LXXIX.

The Author in this Passion seemeth upon mislike of his wearisome estate in love to enter into a deep discourse with himself touching the particular miseries which befall him that loveth. And for his sense in this place, he is very like unto himself, where in a Theme deducted out of the bowels of *Antigone* in Sophocles (which he lately translated into Latin and published in print) he writeth in very like manner as followeth.

Mali quando Cupidinis
Venas aestus edax occupat intimas,
Aretes ingenium labitur in malas;
Iactatur varie, nec Cereris fubit
Nec Bacchi udium; pervigiles trahit
Noctes; cura animum follicita atterit, etc.

And it may appear by the tenor of this Passion that the Author prepareth himself to fall from Love and all his laws, as will well appear by the sequel of his other Passions that follow, which are all made upon this Poesy, *My Love is past.*

Where heat of love doth once possess the heart,
There cares oppress the mind with wondrous ill,
Wit runs awry, not fearing future smart,
And fond desire doth over-master will:
  The belly neither cares for meat nor drink,
  Nor over-watched eyes desire to wink:
Footsteps are false, and wav'ring to and fro;
The brightsome flow'r of beauty fades away:
Reason retires, and pleasure brings in woe:
And wisdom yieldeth place to black decay:
  Counsel, and fame, and friendship are contemn'd:
  And bashful shame, and Gods themselves condemn'd.
Watchful suspect is linked with despair:
Inconstant hope is often drown'd in fears:
What folly hurts, not fortune can repair;
And misery doth swim in Seas of tears:
  Long use of life is but a ling'ring foe,
  And gentle death is only end of woe.

LXXX.

MY LOVE IS PAST.

All such as are but of indifferent capacity, and have some skill in *Arithmetic*, by viewing this Sonnet following compiled by rule and number, into the form of a pillar, may soon judge how much art and study the Author hath bestowed in the same. Wherein as there are placed many pretty observations, so these which I will set down, may be marked for the principal, if any man have such idle leisure to look it over, as the Author had, when he framed it. First therefore it is to be noted that the whole pillar (except the basis or foot thereof) is by relation of either half to the other *Antithetical or Antisyllabical*. Secondly, how this poesy (*Amare est infanire*) runneth twice throughout ye Column, if ye gather but the first letter of every whole verse orderly (excepting the two last) and then in like manner take but the last letter of every one of the said 3 verses, as they stand. Thirdly is to be observed that every verse, but the two last, doth end with the same letter it beginneth, and yet throughout the whole a true time is perfectly observed, although not after our accustomed manner. Fourthly, that the foot of the pillar is *Orchematicall* that is to say, founded by transilition or over-skipping of number by rule and order, as from 1 to 3, 5, 7, and 9; the secret virtue whereof may be learned in Trithemius,(1) as namely by tables of transilition to decipher anything that is written by secret transposition of letters, be it never so cunningly conveyed. And lastly, this observation is not to be neglected, that when all the foresaid particulars as performed, the whole pillar is but just 18 verses, as will appear in the page following it, *Per modum expansionis.*

1. Polygraphiae suae, lib. 5.

LXXXI.

MY LOVE IS PAST.

A Pasquine Piller erected in the despite of Love.

1 At
A 2 last, though
3 late, farewell
4 old well a day : A
m 5 Mirth or mischance strike
a 6 up a newe alarM, And m
7 *Cypria la nemica*
r 8 *miA* Retire to *Cyprus* Isle, a
e 9 and ceafeth thy waRR, Else must thou prove how r
E 10 Reason can by charmE Enforce to flight thy e
s 11 blindfold brat and thee. So frames it with me now, E
t 12 that I confesS, The life I led in *Love* deuoid s / t
I 12 of resT, It was a Hell, where none felt more than I, I
n/s 11 Nor any with like miseries forlorN. Since n
a 10 therefore now my woes are wexed lesS, And s
9 Reason bids me leave old welladA, a
n 8 No longer shall the world laugh me
i 7 to fcorN: I'le choose a path that n
r 6 shall not lead awrie. Rest i
5 then with me from your
4 blind *Cupids* carR r
e. 3 Each one of
2 you, that
1 serve,
3 and would be
5 freE. H'is dooble thrall e.
7 that liu's as Love thinks best, whose
9 hande still Tyrant like to hurt is prefte.(1)

1. Huius Columnae Basis, pro silla- barum numero et linearum proportione est Orchematica..

LXXXII.

MY LOVE IS PAST.
Expansio Columnae praecedentis.

A At last, though late, farewell old wellada; A
m Mirth for mischance strike up a new alarm; m
a And Ciprya *la nemica mia* a
r Retire to Cyprus Ile and cease thy war, r
e Else must thou prove how Reason can by charm e
E Enforce to flight thy blindfold brat and thee. E
s So frames it with me now, that I confess s
t The life I led in Love devoid of rest t
I It was a Hell, where none felt more than I, I
n Nor any with like miseries forlorn. n
s Since therefore now my woes are waxed less, s
a And Reason bids me leave old wellada, a
n No longer shall the world laugh me to scorn: n
i I'll choose a path that shall not lead awry. i
r Rest then with me from your blind Cupid's car r
e Each one of you that serve and would be free. e
His double thrall that Liv's as Love thinks best
Whose hand still Tyrant-like to hurt is press't,

LXXXIII.

MY LOVE IS PAST.

In this Sonnet the Author hath imitated one of Ronsard's *Odes*; which beginneth thus

Les Muses lierent un iour
De chaisnes de roses Amour,[1]
Et pour le garder, le donnerent
Aus Graces et a la Beaute:
Qui voyans so destoyaute,
Sus Parnase l'emprisonnerent, etc.

The Muses not long since entrapping Love
In chains of roses linked all awry,
Gave *Beauty* charge to watch in their behove
With *Graces* three, lest he should wend away:
  Who fearing yet he would escape at last,
  On high Parnassus top they clapp'd him fast.
When Venus understood her Son was thrall,
She made post-haste to have God Vulcan's aid,
Sold him her Gems, and Ceston therewithal,[2]
To ransom home her Son that was betrayed;
  But all in vain, the Muses made no store
  Of gold, but bound him faster than before.
Therefore, all you whom Love did ere abuse,
Come clap your hands with me, to see him thrall,
Whose former deeds no reason can excuse,
For killing those which hurt him not at all:
  Myself by him was lately led awry,
  Though now at last I force my love to die.

1. *Au liure de ses melanges.*
2. V: Martis reuocetur amor, summique Tonantis, A te Juno petat Ceston, et ipsa Venus. Martialis.

LXXXIIII.

MY LOVE IS PAST.

The Author in this Sonnet expresseth his malice towards *Venus* and her Son *Cupid*, by currying favor with Diana, and by suing to have the self same office in her walks and forest, which sometimes her chaste and best-beloved Hippolytus enjoyed. Which *Hippolytus* (as *Servius* witnesseth) died by the false deceit of his Step-mother *Phaedra*, for not yielding over himself unto her incestuous love: whereupon Seneca writeth thus,

Iuuenisque castus crimine incesta iacet,
Pudicus, infons.

Diana, since Hippolytus is dead,
Let me enjoy thy favor, and his place:
My might through will shall stand thee in some stead,
To drive blind Love and Venus from thy chase:
For where they lately wrought me mickle woe,
I vow me now to be their mortal foe.
And do thou not mistrust my chastity
When I shall range amid'st thy virgin train:
My rains are chasten'd so through misery,
That Love with me can nere prevail again:
That The child whose finger once hath felt the fire,
That To play therewith will have but small desire.
Besides, I vow to bear a watchful eye,
Discov'ring such as pass along thy groan;
If Jupiter himself come loit'ring by,
I'll call thy crew and bid them fly from Jove;
For if they stay, he will obtain at last,
What now I loathe, because my love is past.

LXXXV.

MY LOVE IS PAST.

The chiefest substance of this Sonnet is borrowed out of certain Latin verses of Strozza, a nobleman of Italy, and one of the best Poets in all his age: who in describing Metaphorically to his friend Antonius the true form of his amorous estate, writeth thus:

Unda hic sunt Lachrima, Venti supiriae, Remi
Vota, Error vetum, Mens malefana Ratis;
Spes Temo, Curae Comites, Confiantia Amoris
Est malus, Dolor eft Anchora, Nauita Amor, etc.

The soldier worn with wars, delights in peace;
The pilgrim in his ease when toils are past;
The ship to gain the port when storms do cease;
And I rejoice, from Love discharg'd at last;
Whom while I serv'd, peace, rest, and land I lost,
With grievesome wars, with toils, with storms betoss't.
Sweet liberty now gives me leave to sing,
What world it was, where Love the rule did bear;
How foolish Chance by lots rul'd everything;
How *Error* was *mainsail*, each *wave a Tear*; „
The *master*, Love himself; deep *sighs* were *wind*; „
Cares row'd with *vows* the ship *unmerry mind*, „
False hope as *helm* oft turn'd the boat about; „
Inconstant faith stood up for middle mast „
Despair the cable twisted all with Doubt „
Held *Griping Grief* the piked Anchor fast; „
Beauty was all the *rocks*. But I at last, „
Am now twice free, and all my love is past. „

LXXXVI.

MY LOVE IS PAST.

The sense of this Sonnet is for the most part taken out of a letter which *Aeneas Sylvius* wrote unto his friend, to persuade him that albeit he lately had published the wanton love of *Lucretia* and*Euryalus*, yet he liked nothing less than such *fond Love*; and that he now repented him of his own labor over-idly bestowed in describing the same.

Sweet *liberty* restores my wonted joy,
And bids me tell how painters set to view
The form of *Love*. They paint him but a *Boy*,
As working most in minds of youthful crew:
They set him *naked* all, as wanting shame
To keep his secret parts or t'hide the same.
They paint him blind in that he cannot spy
What diff'rence is twixt virtue and default.
With *Bow in hand*, as one that doth defy,
And cumber heedless hearts with fierce assault:
His other hand doth hold a *brand of fire*,
In sign of heat he makes through hot desire.
They give him wings to fly from place to place,
To note that all are wav'ring like the wind,
Whose liberty fond *Love* doth once deface.
This form to *Love* old painters have assign'd:
Whose fond effects if any list to prove,
Where I make end, let them begin to *Love*.

LXXXVII.

MY LOVE IS PAST.

The Author in the first staff of this Sonnet expresseth how Love first went beyond him, by persuading him that all was gold which glistered. In the second, he telleth how time brought him to truth, and Truth to Reason, by whose good counsel he found the way from worse to better, and did overgo the malice of blind Fortune. In the third staff, he craveth pardon at every man for the offenses of his youth; and to Love, the only cause of his long error, he giveth his *ultimum vale.*

Youth made a fault through lightness of Belief,
Which fond Belief Love placed in my breast:
But now I find that Reason gives relief;
And time shows Truth and Wit that's bought is best;
  Muse not therefore although I change my vein,
  He runs too far which never turns again.
Henceforth my mind shall have a watchful eye,
I'll scorn *Fond Love*, and practice of the same:
The wisdom of my heart shall soon descry
Each thing that's good, from what deserveth blame:
  My song shall be; Fortune hath spit her spite,
  And Love can hurt no more withal his might.
Therefore, all you to whom my course is known,
Think better comes, and pardon what is past:
I find that all my wildest Oats are sown,
And joy to see what now I see at last;
  And since that Love was cause I trod awry,
  I here take off his Bells, and let him fly.

LXXXVIII.

MY LOVE IS PAST.

This whole Sonnet is nothing else but a brief and pithy moral, and made after the self same vein with that which is last before it. The two first staffs, (excepting only the two first verses of all) express the Author's alteration of mind and life, and his change from his late vain estate and follies in love, by a metaphor of the ship-man, which by shipwreck's chance is happily restored on a sudden unto that land which he a long time had most wished for.

I long maintained war gainst Reason's rule,
I wander'd pilgrim-like in Error's maze
I sat in Folly's ship, and play'd the fool,
Till on Repentance rock her sides did craze:
   Herewith I learn by hurts already past,
   Till That each extreme will change itself at last.
This shipwreck's chance hath set me on a shelf,
Where neither Love can hurt me any more,
Nor Fortune's hand, though she enforce herself;
Discretion grants to set me safe on shore,
   Where guile is fetter'd fast and wisdom rules,
   To punish heedless hearts and willful fools,
And since the heav'ns have better lot assign'd,
I fear to burn, as having felt the fire;
And proof of harms so changed hath my mind,
That wit and will to Reason do retire:
   Not Venus now, nor love with all his snares
   Can draw my wits to woes at unawares.

LXXXIX.

MY LOVE IS PAST.

The two first staffs of this Sonnet are altogether sentential, and every one verse of them is grounded upon a divers reason and authority from the rest. I have thought good for brevity sake, only to set down here the authorities, with figures, whereby to apply every one of them to his due line in order as they stand. 1. Hieronimus: *In delicijs difficile est seruare castitatem.* 2. Ausonius: *dispulit inconsultus amor etc.* 3. Seneca: *Amor est ociosae causa fellicitudinis.* 4. Propertius: *Errat, qui finem vefani querit amoris.* 5. Horatius: *Semper ardentes acuens sagittas.* 6. Xenophon: *scribit amorem esse igne, et flamma flagrantiorem, quod ignis vrat tangentes, et proxima tantum cremet, amor ex longinquo spectante torreat.* 7. Calenti: *Plurima Zelotipo sunt in amore mala.* 8. Ovidius: *Inferet arma tibi saeua rebellis amor.* 9. Pontanus: *Si vacuum fineret perfidiosus amor.* 10. Marullus: *Quid tantum lachrimis meis proterue Fusultas puer?* 11. Tibullus: *At lasciuis amor rixae mala verba ministrat.* 12. Virgilius: *Bellum foepe petit serus exitiale Cupido.*

Love hath delight in sweet delicious fare;[1]
Love never takes good Counsel for his friend; [2]
Love author is, and cause of idle care; [3]
Love is distraught of wit, and hath no end;[4]
  Love shooteth shafts of burning hot desire;[5]
  Love burneth more than either flame or fire;[6]
Love doth much harm through jealousy's assault;[7]
Love once embrac'd will hardly part again;[8]
Love thinks in breach of faith there is no fault;[9]
Love makes a sport of others' deadly pain;[10]
  Love is a wanton Child and loves to brawl.[11]
  Love with his war brings many souls to thrall.[12]
These are the smallest faults that lurk in Love.
These are the hurts which I have cause to curse,
These are those truths which no man can disprove,
These are such harms as none can suffer worse.
  All this I write, that others may beware,
  Though now myself twice free from all such care.

1. Hieron.
2. Auson.
3. Seneca.
4. Propert.
5. Horat.

6. Xenoph.
7. Calent.
8. Ovid.
9. Pont.
10. Marull.
11. Tibull.
12. Virgil, de Vino et Venere.

XC.

MY LOVE IS PAST.

In this Latin passion, the Author translateth, as it were, paraphrastically the Sonnet of Petrarch, which beginneth thus.

Tennemi Amor anni vent' uno ardendo,[1]
Licto nel foco, e nel duel pien di speme, etc.

But to make it serve his own turn, he varieth from Petrarch's words, where he declareth how many years he lived in love, as well before as since the death of his beloved Laura. Under which name also the Author, in this Sonnet, specifieth her whom he lately loved.

ME sibi ter binos annos unumque subegit
Divus Amor; laetusque sui, licet ignibus arsi;
Spemque habui certam, curis licet ictus acerbis.
Iamgue duos alios exutus amore peregi,
Ac si sydereos mea Laura volarit in orbes,
Duxerit et secum veteris penetralia cordis.
Pertaefum tandem vitae me poenitet actae,
Et pudet erroris pene absumpsisse sub vmbra.
Seminxa virtutum. Sed quae pars vltima restat,
Supplice mente tibi tandem, Deus alte, repono,
Et male transactae deploro tempora vitae,
Cuius agendus erat meliori tramite cursus,
Litis in arcendae sludijs, et pace colendae.
Ergo summe Deus, per quem fum clausus in isto
Carcere, ab aeterno saluum sac esse periclo.

1. Sonnet. 313.

XCI.

MY LOVE IS PAST.

In the latter part of this Sonnet the Author imitateth those verses of Horace.

Me tabula facer
Votiva paries indicat vuida[1]
Suspendise potenti
Vestimenta maris Deo.

Whom also that renowned Florentine M. Agnolo Firenzuela did imitate long ago, both in like manner and matter, as followeth.

O miseri coloro,
Che non prouar di donna fdee mai:
Il pericol, ch'io corsi
Nel tempestoso mar, nella procella
Del lor crudel Amore
Mostrar lo puo la tauoletta posta
E le vesti ancor molli
Sospese all tempio del horrendo Dio
Di questo mar crudele.

Ye captive souls of blindfold *Cyprian's* boat
Mark with advice in what estate ye stand,
Your *Boatman* never whistles merry note,
And Folly keeping stern, still puts from land,
  And makes a sport to toss you to and fro
  Twixt *sighing winds* and surging *waves of woe.*
On *Beauty's* rock she runs you at her will,
And holds you in suspense twixt hope and *fear*,
Where dying oft, yet are you living still,
But such a life as death much better were;
  Be therefore circumspect and follow me,
  When *Chance*, or *change of manners*, sets you free.
Beware how you return to seas again:
Hang up your votive tables in the choir
Of *Cupid's* Church, in witness of the pain
You suffer now by *forced fond desire:*
  Then hang your through-wet garments on the wall,
  And sing with me, *That **Love** is mix'd with gall.*

1. *Ad Pyrrham ode. 5.*

XCII.

MY LOVE IS PAST.

Here the Author by comparing the tyrannous delights and deeds of blind *Cupid* with the honest delights and deeds of other his fellow Goddesses and Gods, doth bless the time and hour that ever he forsook to follow him; whom he confesseth to have been great and forcible in his doings, though but little of stature, and in appearance weakly. Of all the names here mentioned, *Hebe* is seldomest read, wherefore know they which know it not already, that *Hebe* (as Servius writeth) is *Juno's* daughter, having no father, and now wife to *Hercules*, and Goddess of youth and youthly sporting, and was cup-bearer to Jove till she fell in the presence of all the Gods, so unhappily that they saw her privities, whereupon *Jove* being angry, substituted *Ganymedes* into her office and place.

Phoebus delights to view his Laurel Tree;
The Poplar pleaseth Hercules alone;
Melissa mother is, and votrix to the Bee,
Pallas will wear the Olive branch or none;
  Of shepherds and their flock Pallas is Queen;
  And Ceres ripes the corn, was lately green;
To Chloris ev'ry flower belongs of right;
The Dryad Nymphs of woods make chief accompt;
Oreads in hills have their delight;
Diana doth protect each bubbling Fount;
  To Hebe lovely kissing is assign'd;
  To Zephir ev'ry gentle breathing wind.
But what is Love's delight? To hurt each where;
„ He cares not whom, with darts of deep desire;
„ With watchful jealousy, with hope, with fear,
„ With nipping cold and secret flames of fire.
    O happy hour wherein I did forego
    This little God, so great a cause of woe.

XCIII.

MY LOVE IS PAST.

In the first and sixth line of this Passion the Author alludeth to two sententious verses in Sophocles

In the other two staffs following, the Author pursueth on his matter, beginning and ending every line with the self same syllable he used in the first: wherein he imitateth some Italian Poets, who more to try their wits than for any other conceit, have written after the like manner.

My love is past, woe worth the day and *hour*
When to such folly first I did *incline*,
Whereof the very thought is bitter *sour*,
And still would hurt, were not my soul *divine*,
  Or did not Reason teach that care in *vain*
  For ill once past, which cannot turn *again*.
My Love is past, blessed the day and *hour*.
When from so fond estate I did *decline*,
Wherein was little sweet with mickle *sour,*
And loss of mind, whose substance is divine.
  Or at the left, expense of time in *vain*,
  For which expense no ***Love*** returneth *gain*.
My ***Love*** is past, wherein was no *good hour:*
When others joy'd, to cares I did *incline*,
Whereon I fed, although the taste were *sour*,
And still believ'd Love was some pow'r *divine*,
  Or some instinct which could not work in *vain*,
  Forgetting, Time well spent was double *gain*.

1. In Oedipo-Colonae.
2. In Trachiniis.

XCIIII.

MY LOVE IS PAST.

In this Passion the Author hath but augmented the invention of Seraphine, where he writeth in this manner.

Biastemo quando mai le labbra apersi
Per dar name a costei, che accid me induce.
Biastemo il tempo, e quanti giorni ho persi
A seguitar si tenebrosa luce:
Biastemo charta, inchiostre, e versi,
Et quanto Amor per me fama gliaduce;
Biastemo quando mai la vidi anchora,
El mese, l'anno, e giorno, el punto, e lhora.

I Curse the time, wherein these lips of mine
Did pray or praise the Dame that was unkind:
I curse both leaf, and ink, and every line
My hand hath writ, in hope to move her mind:
  I curse her hollow heart and flatt'ring eyes,
  Whose sly deceit did cause my mourning cries:
I curse the sugar'd speech and Siren's song,
Wherewith so oft she hath bewitch'd mine ear:
I curse my foolish will, that stay'd so long,
And took delight to bide twixt hope and fear:
  I curse the hour wherein I first began
  By loving looks to prove a witless man:
I curse those days which I have spent in vain,
By serving such an one as recks no right:
I curse each cause of all my secret pain,
Though Love to hear the same have small delight:
  And since the heav'ns my freedom now restore,
  Henceforth I'll live at ease, and love no more.

XCV.

MY LOVE IS PAST.

A *Labyrinth* is a place made full of turnings and creeks, where hence, he that is once gotten in can hardly get out again. Of this sort *Pliny* (1) mentioneth four in the world which were most noble. One in *Crete* made by *Daedalus*, at the commandment of king *Minos*, to shut up the *Minotaur* in: to which monster the *Athenians* by league were bound every year to send seven of their children, to be devoured; which was performed till at the last, by the help of *Ariadne*, Theseus slew the monster. Another he mentioneth to have been in *Egypt*, which also *Pomponius Mela* describeth in his first book. The third in *Lemnos*, wherein were erected a hundred and fifty pillars of singular workmanship. The fourth in Italy, builded by *Porsenna* king of *Etruria*, to serve for his sepulcher. But in this Passion the Author alludeth unto that of *Crete* only.

Though somewhat late, at last I found the way
To leave the doubtful Labyrinth of *Love*,
Wherein (alas) each minute seem'd a day:
Himself was *Minotaur*; whose force to prove
  I was enforc'd, till Reason taught my mind
  To stay the beast, and leave him there behind.
But being scaped thus from out his maze,
And past the dang'rous Den so full of doubt,
False Theseus-like, my credit shall I craze,
Forsaking her whose hand did help me out?
  With *Ariadne Reason* shall not say,
  I *sav'd his life, and yet he runs away.*
No, no, before I leave the golden rule,
Or laws of her that stood so much my friend,
Or once again will play the loving fool,
The sky shall fall, and all shall have an end:
I wish as much to you that lovers be,
Whose pains will pass, if you beware by me.

1. Lib 36. ca. 13.

XCVI.

MY LOVE IS PAST.

In this Passion, the Author in scoffing bitterly at Venus and her son Cupid, alludeth unto certain verses in Ovid, but inverteth them to another sense than Ovid used, who wrote them upon the death of Tibullus. These are the verses which he imitateth,

Ecce puer Veneris sert everfamque pharetram,
Et fractos arcus, et fine luce facem,
Ad spice demissis ut eat miserabilis alis,[1]
Pectoraque insesta tondat aperta manu, etc.
Nec minus est confusa Venus, etc.
Quam inuuenis rupit cum serus inguen aper.

What ails poor Venus now to sit alone
In funeral attire, her wonted hue
Quite chang'd, her smile to tears, her mirth to moan:
As though Adonis' wounds now bled anew,
  Or she with young Julus late return'd
  From seeing her Aeneas' carcass burn'd.
Alack for woe, what ails her little Boy,
To have his tender cheeks besprent with tears,
And sit and sigh, where he was wont to toy?
How haps, no longer he his quiver wears,
  But breaks his Bow, throwing the *shivers by,
  And plucks his wings and lets his firebrand die?
No, Dame and Darling too, ye come too late,
To win me now, as you have done tofore:
I live secure and quiet in estate,
Fully resolv'd from loving any more:
  Go pack for shame from hence to Cyprus Ile,
  And there go play your pranks another while.

1. Elegiar. lib. 1

XCVII.

MY LOVE IS PAST.

The Author in this passion alludeth to the fable of Phineus which is set down at large in the *Argonautics* of Apollonius, and Valerius Flaccus. He compareth himself unto Phineus, his Mistress unto the Harpies; and his thoughts unto Zetes, and his desires unto Calais, the two twins of Boreas; and the voice of Ne plus vltra spoken from Heaven to Calais and Zetes, unto the *Divine grace*, which willed him to follow no further the miseries of a Lover's estate, but to profess unfeignedly that his Love is past. And last of all, the Author concludeth against the sour sauce of Love with the French proverb: *Pour un plaisir mille douleurs.*

The Harpy birds that did in such despite
Grieve and annoy old Phineus so sore,
Where chas'd away by Calais in flight
And by his brother Zetes for evermore;
  Who follow'd them until they heard on high
  A voice, that said, Ye Twins No further fly.
Phineus I am, that so tormented was;
My Laura here I may an Harpy name;
My thoughts and lusts be Sons to Boreas,
Which never ceas'd in following my Dame,
  Till heav'nly Grace said unto me at last,
  Leave fond Delights, and say thy love is past.
My love is past I say, and sing full glad;
My time, alas, misspent in Love I rue,
Wherein few joys, or none at all I had,
But store of woes: I found the proverb true,
  For ev'ry pleasure that in *Love* is found,
  A thousand woes and more therein abound.

XCVIII.

MY LOVE IS PAST.

The Author in this passion, telling what Love is, easeth his heart, as it were, by railing outright where he can work no other manner of revenge. The invention hereof, for the most part of the particulars contained, is taken out of certain Latin verses which this Author composed upon *Quid Amor.* Which because they may well import a passion of the writer, and aptly befit the present title of his over-passed Love, he setteth them down in this next page following, but not as accomptable for one of the hundred passions of this book.

Hark wanton youths, whom Beauty maketh blind,
And learn of me what kind a thing is *Love*;
Love is a Brain-sick Boy, and fierce by kind;
A Willful Thought, which Reason can not move;
A Flatt'ring Sycophant; a Murd'ring Thief;
A Poison'd choking Bait; a Ticing Grief;
A Tyrant in his Laws; in speech untrue;
A Blindfold Guide; a Feather in the wind;
A right Chameleon for change of hue; [1]
A Lame-limb *Lust*; a Tempest of the mind;
A Breach of Chastity; all virtues' Foe;
A Private war; A Toilsome web of woe;
A Fearful jealousy; a Vain Desire;
A *Labyrinth*; a Pleasing *Misery*;
A Shipwracke of man's life; a Smokeless fire;
A Sea of tears; a lasting *Lunacy*;
A Heavy servitude; a Dropsy Thirst;
A Hellish Gale, whose captives are accurst.

1. Vide Plin natura. Hist. lib. 28. cap. 8.

MY LOVE IS PAST.

Quid Amor?

Quid sit amor, qualisque, cupis me scire magistro?
Est Veneris proles: coelo metuendus, et Orco;
Et leuior ventis; et fulminis ocyor alis;
Peruigil excubitor; fallax comes; inuidus hospes;
Armatus puer; infanus iuuenis; novitatis
Quesitor, belli fautor; virtuti inimicus;
Splendidus ore, nocens promisso; lege tyrannus;
Dux caecus; gurges viciorum; noctus alumnus;
Fur clandestinus; mors viuida; mortua vita;
Dulcis inexpertis, expertis durus; Eremus
Stultitiae; facula ignescens; vesana libido;
Zelotypum frigus; mala mens; corrupta voluntas;
Pluma leuis; morbus iecoris; dementia prudens;
Infamis leno; Bacchi, Cererisque minister;
Prodiga libertas animae; Pruritus inanis;
Prauorum carcer; Corrupti sanguinis ardor;
Irrationalis motus; sycophanta bilinguis;
Struma pudicitiae; sumi expers flamma; patronus
Periuroe linguae; prostrato foeuus; amicus
Immeritis; animi tempestas; luxuriosus
Praeceptor, fine fine malum; fine pace duellum;
Naufragium humanie vitae; loethale venenum;
Flebile cordolium; grave calcar; acuta fagitta;
Sontica pernicies, nodofoe causa podagrae;
Natus ad infidias vulpes: pontus lachrymarum;
Virgineae Zonae ruptura; dolosa voluptas;
Multicolor serpens; vrens affectus; inermis
Bellator; fenijque caput, feniumque iuuentae?
Ante diem funus; portantis vipera; moestus
Pollinctor; syren fallax; mors proeuia morti;
Infector nemorum; erroris Labyrinthus; amara
Dulcedo; inuentor falsi; via perditionis;
Formarum egregius spectator; poena perennis;
Suspirans ventus; singultu plena querela;
Triste magisterium; multae iactura diei;
Martyrium innocui; temerarius aduena; pondus
Sisyphium; radix curarum; defidis esta;
Febris anhela; fitis moroa; hidropicus ardor;
Vis uno dicam verbo? incarnata Gehenna est.

XCIX.

MY LOVE IS PAST.

This passion is an imitation of the first Sonnet in Seraphine, and grounded upon that which Aristotle writeth of the Eagle,[1] for the proof she maketh of her birds, by setting them to behold the Sun. After whom Pliny hath written, as followeth:

Aquila implumes etiamnum pullos suos percutiens, Subinde cogit adversos intueri Solis radios: et si conniventum humectantemque animadvertit, praecipitat e nido,velut adulterinum atque degenerem: illum, cuius acies firma contra steterit, educat. [2]

The haughty Eagle Bird, of Birds the best,
Before the feathers of her younglings grow,
She lifts them one by one from out their nest,
To view the Sun, thereby her own to know;
Those that behold it not with open eye,
She lets them fall, not able yet to fly.
Such was my case, when *Love* possess'd my mind;
Each thought of mine, which could not bide the light
Of her my Sun, whose beams had made me blind,
I made my Will suppress it with *Despite*:
But such a thought as could abide her best,
I harbor'd still within my careful breast.
But those fond days are past and half forgot;
I practice now the quite clean contrary:
What thoughts can like of her, I like them not,
But choke them straight, for fear of jeopardy;
For thou that *Love* to some do seem a Toy;
I know by proof that *Love* is long annoy.

1. Lib. 9 Hist. animal.
2. Nat. Hist. Lib. 10. cap. 1.

C.

MY LOVE IS PAST.

The Author feigneth here that *Love*, essaying with his brand to fire the heart of some such Lady on whom it would not work immediately, to try whether the old virtue of it were extinguished or no, applied it unto his own breast, and thereby foolishly consumed himself. This invention hath some relation unto the Epitaph of *Love*, written by M. Girolimo *Parabosco*;

In cenere giace qui sepolto Amore,
Colpa di quella, chemorir mi face, etc.

Resolv'd to dust entomb'd here lieth *Love*,
Through fault of her, who here herself should lie;
He struck her breast, but all in vain did prove
To fire the ice: and doubting by and by
  His brand had lost his force, he gan to try
  Upon himself; which trial made him die.
In sooth no force; let those lament who lust,
I'll find a carol song for obsequy;
For towards me his dealings were unjust,
And cause of all my passed misery:
  The Fates, I think, seeing what I had past,
  In my behalf wrought this revenge at last.
But somewhat more to pacify my mind,
By illing him, through whom I liv'd a slave,
I'll cast his ashes to the open wind,
Or write this Epitaph upon his grave;

Here lieth Love, of Mars the bastard Son,
V Vhose foolish fault to death himself hath done.

MY LOVE IS PAST.

This is an Epilogue to the whole work, and more like a prayer than a Passion: and is faithfully translated out of Petrarch, Sonnet. 314. 2. part, where he beginneth,

I vo piangendo i mici passati tempi
I quai posi in amar cosa mortale,
Senza leuarmi a volo, lauena iosempi, etc.
Per dar forse di me non bassi essempi, etc.

Lugeo iam querulus vitae tot lustra peracta,
 Quae male consumpsi, mortalia vana secutur,
 Cum tamen alatus potue volitasse per altum,
 Exemplarque suisse aliis, nec inutile forsan.
Tu mea qui peccata vides, culpasque nefandas,
 Coeli summe parens, magnum, et venerabile numen,
 Collapsae succurre animae; mentisque caducae
 Candida defectum tua gratia suppleat omnem.
Ut, qui sustinui bellum, durasque procellas,
 In pace, et portu moriar: minimeque probanda
 Si mea cita suit, tamen ut claudatur honeste.
Tantillo vitae spacio, quod sort supersit,
 Funeribusque, meis praesentim porrige dextram;
 Ipse vides, in te quam spes mea tota reposta est.

F I N I S.

The Labor is light, where Love is the Paymistress

Also from Benediction Books ...

Wandering Between Two Worlds: Essays on Faith and Art
Anita Mathias
Benediction Books, 2007
152 pages
ISBN: 0955373700

Available from www.amazon.com, www.amazon.co.uk
www.wanderingbetweentwoworlds.com

In these wide-ranging lyrical essays, Anita Mathias writes, in lush, lovely prose, of her naughty Catholic childhood in Jamshedpur, India; her large, eccentric family in Mangalore, a sea-coast town converted by the Portuguese in the sixteenth century; her rebellion and atheism as a teenager in her Himalayan boarding school, run by German missionary nuns, St. Mary's Convent, Nainital; and her abrupt religious conversion after which she entered Mother Teresa's convent in Calcutta as a novice. Later rich, elegant essays explore the dualities of her life as a writer, mother, and Christian in the United States-- Domesticity and Art, Writing and Prayer, and the experience of being "an alien and stranger" as an immigrant in America, sensing the need for roots.

About the Author

Anita Mathias was born in India, has a B.A. and M.A. in English from Somerville College, Oxford University and an M.A. in Creative Writing from the Ohio State University. Her essays have been published in The Washington Post, The London Magazine, The Virginia Quarterly Review, Commonweal, Notre Dame Magazine, America, The Christian Century, Religion Online, The Southwest Review, Contemporary Literary Criticism, New Letters, The Journal, and two of HarperSanFrancisco's The Best Spiritual Writing anthologies. Her non-fiction has won fellowships from The National Endowment for the Arts; The Minnesota State Arts Board; The Jerome Foundation, The Vermont Studio Center; The Virginia Centre for the Creative Arts, and the First Prize for the Best General Interest Article from the Catholic Press Association of the United States and Canada. Anita has taught Creative Writing at the College of William and Mary, and now lives and writes in Oxford, England.

The Greater Trumps, Charles Williams

My Apprenticeship: Volumes I and II, Beatrice Webb

Last and First Men / Star Maker, Olaf Stapledon

Last and First Men, Olaf Stapledon

Darkness and the Light, Olaf Stapledon

The Worst Journey in the World, Apsley Cherry-Garrard

The Schoole of Abuse, Containing a Pleasaunt Invective Against Poets, Pipers, Plaiers, Iesters and Such Like Catepillers of the Commonwelth, Stephen Gosson

Russia in the Shadows, H. G. Wells

Wild Swans at Coole, W. B. Yeats

A hundreth good pointes of husbandrie, Thomas Tusser

The Collected Works of Nathanael West: "The Day of the Locust", "The Dream Life of Balso Snell", "Miss Lonelyhearts", "A Cool Million", Nathanael West

Miss Lonelyhearts & The Day of the Locust, Nathaniel West

The Worst Journey in the World, Apsley Cherry-Garrard

Scott's Last Expedition, V1, R. F. Scott

The Dream of Gerontius, John Henry Newman

The Brother of Daphne, Dornford Yates

The Downfall of Robert Earl of Huntington, Anthony Munday

Clayhanger, Arnold Bennett

The Regent, A Five Towns Story Of Adventure In London , Arnold Bennett

The Card, A Story Of Adventure In The Five Towns , Arnold Bennett

South: The Story of Shackleton's Last Expedition 1914-1917, Sir Ernest Shackketon

Greene's Groatsworth of Wit: Bought With a Million of Repentance, Robert Greene

Beau Sabreur, Percival Christopher Wren

The Hekatompathia, or Passionate Centurie of Love, Thomas Watson

The Art of Rhetoric, Thomas Wilson

Stepping Heavenward, Elizabeth Prentiss

Barker's Delight, or The Art of Angling, Thomas Barker

The Napoleon of Notting Hill, G.K. Chesterton

The Douay-Rheims Bible (The Challoner Revision)

Endimion - The Man in the Moone, John Lyly

Gallathea and Midas, John Lyly,

Mother Bombie, John Lyly

Manners, Custom and Dress During the Middle Ages and During the Renaissance Period, Paul Lacroix

Obedience of a Christian Man, William Tyndale

St. Patrick for Ireland, James Shirley

The Wrongs of Woman; Or Maria/Memoirs of the Author of a Vindication of the Rights of Woman, Mary Wollstonecraft and William Godwin

De Adhaerendo Deo. Of Cleaving to God, Albertus Magnus

Obedience of a Christian Man, William Tyndale

A Trick to Catch the Old One, Thomas Middleton

The Phoenix, Thomas Middleton

A Yorkshire Tragedy, Thomas Middleton (attrib.)

The Princely Pleasures at Kenelworth Castle, George Gascoigne

The Fair Maid of the West. Part I and Part II. Thomas Heywood

Proserpina, Volume I and Volume II. Studies of Wayside Flowers, John Ruskin

Our Fathers Have Told Us. Part I. The Bible of Amiens. John Ruskin

The Poetry of Architecture: Or the Architecture of the Nations of Europe Considered in Its Association with Natural Scenery and National Character, John Ruskin

The Endeavour Journal of Sir Joseph Banks. Sir Joseph Banks

Christ Legends: And Other Stories, Selma Lagerlof; (trans. Velma Swanston Howard)

Chamber Music, James Joyce

Blurt, Master Constable, Thomas Middleton, Thomas Dekker

Since Yesterday, Frederick Lewis Allen

The Scholemaster: Or, Plaine and Perfite Way of Teachyng Children the Latin Tong , Roger Ascham

The Wonderful Year, 1603, Thomas Dekker

Waverley, Sir Walter Scott

Guy Mannering, Sir Walter Scott

Old Mortality, Sir Walter Scott

The Knight of Malta, John Fletcher

The Double Marriage, John Fletcher and Philip Massinger

Space Prison, Tom Godwin

The Home of the Blizzard Being the Story of the Australasian Antarctic Expedition, 1911-1914, Douglas Mawson

Wild-goose Chase , John Fletcher

If You Know Not Me, You Know Nobody. Part I and Part II, Thomas Heywood

The Ragged Trousered Philanthropists, Robert Tressell

The Island of Sheep, John Buchan

Eyes of the Woods, Joseph Altsheler

The Club of Queer Trades, G. K. Chesterton

The Financier, Theodore Dreiser

Something of Myself, Rudyard Kipling

Law of Freedom in a Platform, or True Magistracy Restored, Gerrard Winstanley

Damon and Pithias, Richard Edwards

Dido Queen of Carthage: And, The Massacre at Paris, Christopher Marlowe

Cocoa and Chocolate: Their History from Plantation to Consumer, Arthur Knapp

Lady of Pleasure, James Shirley

The South Pole: An account of the Norwegian Antarctic expedition in the "Fram," 1910-12. Volume 1 and Volume 2, Roald Amundsen

A Yorkshire Tragedy, Thomas Middleton (attrib.)

The Tragedy of Soliman and Perseda, Thomas Kyd

The Rape of Lucrece. Thomas Heywood

Myths and Legends of Ancient Greece and Rome, E. M. Berens

In the Forbidden Land, Henry Savage Arnold Landor

Across Unknown South America, by Arnold Henry Savage Landor

Illustrated History of Furniture: From the Earliest to the Present Time, Frederick Litchfield

A Narrative of Some of the Lord's Dealings with George Müller Written by Himself (Parts I-IV, 1805-1856), George Müller

The Towneley Cycle Of The Mystery Plays (Or The Wakefield Cycle): Thirty-Two Pageants, Anonymous

The Insatiate Countesse, John Marston.

Spontaneous Activity in Education, Maria Montessori.

On the Art of Writing, Sir Arthur Quiller-Couch

The Well of the Saints, J. M. Synge

Bacon's Advancement Of Learning And The New Atlantis, Francis Bacon.

Catholic Tales And Christian Songs, Dorothy Sayers.

Two Little Savages: Being the Adventures of Two Boys who Lived as Indians and What they Learned, Ernest Thompson Seton

The Sadness of Christ, Thomas More

The Family of Love, Thomas Middleton

The Passing of the Aborigines: A Lifetime Spent Among the Natives of Australia, Daisy Bates

The Children, Edith Wharton

www.ingramcontent.com/pod-product-compliance
Lightning Source LLC
Chambersburg PA
CBHW031301060726
47590CB00003B/1002

* 9 7 8 1 8 4 9 0 2 1 2 3 4 *